Citizens to Arms!

Uniforms of the French Revolutionary Armies 1792–1799

Yves Martin

Helion & Company

**To Robert K. Pye and Hans-Karl Weiss,
yours for the French Revolution!**

Helion & Company Limited
Unit 8 Amherst Business Centre
Budbrooke Road
Warwick
CV34 5WE
England
Tel. 01926 499619
Email: info@helion.co.uk
Website: www.helion.co.uk
X (formerly Twitter): @Helionbooks
Facebook: @HelionBooks
Visit our blog at http://blog.helion.co.uk/

Published by Helion & Company 2024
Designed and typeset by Mach 3 Solutions (www.mach3solutions.co.uk)
Cover designed by Paul Hewitt, Battlefield Design (www.battlefield-design.co.uk)

Text © Yves Martin 2024
Illustrations © as individually credited
Colour plates and cover: A series of gouaches by Henry Boisselier, 1943, from the author's collection

Every reasonable effort has been made to trace copyright holders and to obtain their permission for the use of copyright material. The author and publisher apologise for any errors or omissions in this work, and would be grateful if notified of any corrections that should be incorporated in future reprints or editions of this book.

ISBN 978-1-804515-42-6

British Library Cataloguing-in-Publication Data.
A catalogue record for this book is available from the British Library.

All rights reserved. No part of this publication may be reproduced, stored in a retrieval system, or transmitted, in any form, or by any means, electronic, mechanical, photocopying, recording or otherwise, without the express written consent of Helion & Company Limited.

For details of other military history titles published by Helion & Company Limited, contact the above address, or visit our website: http://www.helion.co.uk

We always welcome receiving book proposals from prospective authors.

Contents

Introduction: How Citizens Became Soldiers — iv

1 Henry Boisselier, the Man and his Work — 7
2 'Forward, children of the fatherland!' – True Tales of Volunteers — 11
3 The Plates — 19
4 Conclusion — 142

Sources, Bibliography, and Further Reading — 144

Introduction
How Citizens Became Soldiers

On 20 April 1792, the French Revolutionary government declared war on the 'King of Hungary and Bohemia' (i.e. Francis I of Austria). This was the starting point of close to 23 years of continuous conflict within Europe.

This was the far-reaching consequence of events which had unfolded three years before. The storming of the Bastille prison by a revolutionary mob on 14 July 1789 is commonly seen as the beginning of the 'French Revolution', yet this was just the culmination of many problems and unrest which had plagued the French kingdom since the end of the American War of Independence in 1783.

Between 1789 and 1792, much was done to reform the kingdom and put in place a constitutional monarchy similar to that existing in Great Britain. However, as political events unfolded pro-reform and anti-reform parties became locked into deadly opposition.

The European powers looked on at the collapse of the French monarchy, mostly in horror and fearing similar events in their own countries. Great Britain was an exception, as they initially viewed the French revolution in a positive light. For Great Britain, it meant that its main continental enemy was weakened by political chaos but also that it was moving, politically and socially, in a direction which could bring about better understanding between the two nations. However, the rest of the European monarchies had a very unfavourable view of events. Francis I of Austria, both as an absolute monarch and as the brother of the French queen could not accept the increasing radicalisation of the Revolutionary government. Accordingly, Austria and Prussia formed a coalition on 7 February 1792. Although its main aim was against the vanishing kingdom of Poland, it was perceived in France as an anti-French move intended to attack the revolutionaries.

The French army which engaged in the conflict was still the old royal army. Apart from a few changes made in 1791, it was dressed according to the royal regulation of 1786. The infantry was dressed in white, and regiments had just traded their traditional names for a numbering system. By the end of May 1792, three cavalry regiments: the Royal-Allemand, Bercheny, and Saxe hussars all deserted to the enemy, or rather joined the counter-revolutionary émigré forces which were being assembled just across the Rhine alongside the Prussian and Austrian forces.

The need for both fresh and reliable troops was quickly felt by the French government and 'volunteers' were called upon to fight to save the revolutionary movement. In the eastern border areas of France, spirits ran high and on 25 April 1792 a little-known officer in the engineers garrisoned in Strasbourg, Rouget de l'Isle, at the request of hothead patriots composed a song: 'the war song for the army of the Rhine'. L'Isle sang it for the first time with the mayor of Strasburg as his main audience, while the mayor's wife played the tune on her pianoforte. A few months later, as a group of volunteers from Marseilles arrived in Paris, they sang this very same song, which was quickly adopted by the French people and became known as *La Marseillaise* (the Marseilles song). Its catchy tune pleased all ears while its violent yet patriotic words matched the volunteers' mood: 'aux armes citoyens!' – citizens to arms!

Within a matter of months, the French army under this influx of volunteers was to change drastically. Many units were raised, most of them ill-trained, ill-equipped and all too often proved to be just ill-disciplined rabble. Yet, during 1792–1795 these 'volunteers' were gradually forged into an effective fighting force which survived its initial defeats and became foundation of the future victorious Revolutionary armies. From these, a young ambitious and gifted general who was the hero of Toulon, would eventually be able to seize supreme power in France and build the first Grande armée which would achieve fame at the battles of Austerlitz, Iena and many more.

On numerous occasions, during the 1792–1802 period, Republican France had to fight not only for its survival on all its borders, but also internally due to the various counter-revolutionary insurrections in the west of the country (the Vendee) as well as in Lyon, Toulon, and other places. In many cases, the Revolutionary government in Paris had to raise forces locally to cope with these internal uprisings.

This work deals with the troops which composed the French Revolutionary armies. It cannot however be an exhaustive work, giving all details on every single unit which existed and its wide variety of uniforms. This is simply impossible given how much improvisation went into raising these units and the fact that information on them was not always documented, and all too often when it existed it may not have survived.

The one and only base for this work is a series of fine gouaches done by the talented artist Henry Boisselier in 1943. This body of work was most probably a commission for a private collector, Albert Depréaux, whose name appears as a pencil note on the back of one plate. As such it presents a fairly comprehensive modern artistic representation of the various types of Revolutionary troops which existed between 1792 and approximately 1800. Boisselier starts his series covering the former royal units and ends with the late Directorate period just before Napoleon Bonaparte seized power. Accordingly, the opening chapter deals with Henry Boisselier, his work and the little that can be said of this specific series in terms of sources and the execution of his work.

As the bulk of this volume is related to the analysis of each plate in the Boisselier series, it seemed inappropriate and of little added value to provide a history of the Revolutionary Wars. The reader can refer to the multiple works related to this topic. However, iconographic representations of the citizen soldiers, even as colourful and lively as Boisselier's can hardly convey who those men were. Rather than provide a lengthy and academic discussion on their mind-sets, feelings and moral attitude, the author has decided to focus on 'true tales' of volunteers which are presented in the second chapter.

The third, and largest chapter of this volume, is devoted to an analysis of each of the Boisselier plates. Each plate's legend is aimed at being as self-sufficient and exhaustive as possible, which may imply some repetition. The reader can however just look up any given plate to find relevant information, such as its context and sources used.

At the end of the book there is a section that deals with sources used to create this volume and a respective bibliography. The overall aim is to give the reader both the usual listing of the main works used, but also to encourage them into further reading, and most importantly to encourage others to pursue further research.

Hopefully, this work will be appreciated by all lovers of military history, especially those who focus on the Napoleonic period (1789–1815). The Revolutionary period uniforms are typically less well known, yet they were the blueprints for the later imperial dress. They also offer a great variety in terms of colour while often cutting an attractive unusual figure.

As always, this work could not have happened without the help of many. My dear wife's patience towers above all other support, as she calmly accepted both the time required for writing but also the piles of documents which invaded our comfortable but always too small Parisian abode. My old and dear friends at the various French military history associations – La Sabretache, Le Briquet, and Le Bivouac – have all been instrumental over the years, as have so many others with whom I have exchanged via electronic mail or social media.

Finally, I wish to acknowledge the debt I owe to two great enthusiasts whose works on the Revolutionary period were an inspiration and a source but who have unfortunately passed away even before this was even a project. Both are sorely missed.

Bernard Coppens, wonderful artist and brilliant historian, with whom I exchanged on many topics and had, like me, a true love and passion for the 'revolutionaries'.

Didier Davin, President of Le Bivouac, with whom I sometimes exchanged but never had the pleasure to meet. His wonderfully detailed articles on these many odd and little-known Revolutionary units remain a reference.

As always…

Salut et fraternité!

Yves Martin
Paris, 30 Nivôse An 232

1

Henry Boisselier, the Man and his Work

Until the late 1990s and early 2000s, few collectors and hobbyists knew the name of Henry Boisselier. Enthusiasts, eager for documentation on uniforms, generally relied upon the great works done by Rousselot, Leliepvre, RIGO, and Girbal. These four great artists have come to dominate the second half of the twentieth century. They each published detailed plates and their works were often featured in military themed magazines which had started appearing in the 1960s, like *Tradition* (UK) and later in France, *Uniformes*, *Tradition* (France), as well as others.

With the publication in the late 1970s and early 1980s of Bucquoy's First Empire uniform postcards in book format, Boisselier's name appeared but his contribution to that series did not generate as much enthusiasm as Benigni's superb series on the guard cavalry or cuirassiers.

Indeed, unlike the four artists mentioned above, Boisselier had published very little in his lifetime. Even some of his direct contemporaries like Maurice Toussaint or Pierre-Albert Leroux had contributed to various books, illustrations and even come up with plate series.

However, many 'old collectors' were the only ones who actually knew how much Boisselier had produced and how much he had contributed to the knowledge of military uniforms. In large part this was due to the fact that Boisselier mainly worked on private commissions, and it remains an impossible task to list all the plates produced during his lifetime. Since the late 1990s, the advent of new technologies such as high-resolution digital scanning along with quality colour image processing and reproduction has enabled the sharing of many of Boisselier's works which have come to light through antiquarians and private auctions.

Yet, despite how much Boisselier contributed to our knowledge of military uniforms, we know fairly little about the man himself. The main written source on his life is his obituary featured in the November 1959 bulletin of the Société des collectionneurs de figurines historiques. Boisselier

Henry Boisselier. (La Sabretache archives)

had been a regular contributor to those bulletins over the past 10 years, usually providing them with simple black and white plates, sometimes devoted to a full study like the cavalry of the Cisalpine Republic and Kingdom of Italy, the Paris Garde nationale in 1814, or 1870–1871 French uniforms. In addition to this one formal document, the author has been able to gather various anecdotes from 'old timers' who knew Boisselier personally, and now pass them on to younger generations of enthusiasts.

Boisselier was born on 13 April 1881, to an old Parisian family which could trace its presence in the capital to the regency period of the 1720s. The Boisselier family was always active as craftsmen or artists. Thus, Boisselier attended the prestigious École Boulle which to this day remains the top school for professional craftsmen. After graduation he was a metal engraver for a few years.

Boisselier had always been interested in military history and uniforms. It is said that his father had played an active role in the 1870 Franco-Prussian war as a national guard. This also determined his keen interest in the Second Empire and that specific conflict on which he gathered massive and precise documentation. Some of his best work is related to it.

In the early 1900s, the world of militaria enthusiasts was quite active in Paris. The La Sabretache association was founded in 1893 with the goal of creating a national army museum. This rather exclusive club brought together both representatives of upper society interested in military matters (a quite popular topic in post 1870 France) as well as young researchers and collectors, military or civilian. The bulletin they produced, *le carnet de la Sabretache*, was a treasure trove of information of all kinds. Another publication from that period was *La Giberne* (the cartridge box) published by Louis Fallou. Fallou was both an enthusiast and an antiquarian by trade. He was a self-educated man who produced this high-quality magazine with the purpose of providing both documentation and supporting his own antiques trading. Another major character of the period was young gendarmerie *capitaine*, Eugène Louis Bucquoy, who was fascinated by understanding what soldiers of the past truly wore. Over time, Bucquoy was to become one of the founding fathers of French uniforms research, especially as he embarked on a mammoth project: an encyclopaedia of French uniforms worn during the Revolutionary and imperial periods. For this Bucquoy used the fairly simple and then very popular medium of postcards. Starting in 1906, he drew and painted the first series. These were well received despite their very poor artistic quality. Given this, Bucquoy started bringing together various art contributors, one of which was Boisselier who produced his first series (the 2e conscrits-chasseurs de la garde) in 1910. This contribution continued throughout the Bucquoy cards series. Indeed, one of the last (the guard grenadiers) was by Boisselier and published in 1944. The two men not only collaborated on the cards, but also on the other major Bucquoy production: *Le Passepoil* which was both a club and a bulletin which started publishing in 1921. Boisselier was one of its most regular contributors. *Le Passepoil* focused mainly on periods and uniforms other than the revolution and First Empire. Thanks to the cards and *Passepoil*, Boisselier's reputation extended beyond France. He was in contact with Herbert Knötel der Junge in Germany, Reverend Percy White in the United Kingdom, Italo Cenni in Italy, and others. He also produced some Brauer-Bogen and Grosse Uniformenkunde Neue Folge plates for Knötel. These international contacts provided him with quality information on non-French armies of all periods which helped him produce plates on such scarce topics for his various clients.

The above sums up the published production from Boisselier, which was therefore limited to Bucquoy postcards and a few plates. As stated, Boisselier's main production was for private collectors who wanted plates and even full series to help them document uniforms either for their own knowledge or to help them have their large flat figures collections painted.

From the 1910s all the way up to his death on 15 September 1959, Boisselier produced hundreds, if not thousands, of plates on a wide variety of military topics. Although the French army was, of course his main focus, his international network enabled him to offer to his clients a variety of offerings as diverse as the armies of the confederation of the Rhine, the British army of 1812–1815, and even scarcer French topics such as French marine and colonial troops, the army of Africa, or the army in Egypt.

Boisselier had an uncanny gift that all those who met him remember. He could outperform anyone in terms of speed when drawing or painting. He could produce a detailed sketch in a matter of a few minutes. A simple not too elaborate watercolour plate could take him only a quarter of an hour to achieve. This speed helped him copy all kinds of contemporary and original works he would see in collections, museums, libraries, auctions, or even when displayed in a bookdealer's window. The story goes that he had seen the famous *Camp de Dresde* manuscript formerly in Detaille's possession on display at a famous antiquarian's on the boulevard Saint-Germain. He bribed the young shop attendant so that she would turn each page every 10 minutes, and so by the end of the day Boisselier went home with his own personal copy of the manuscript.

Unlike many other artists, Boisselier was keen to precisely document each plate he was doing. There are very few exceptions to this rule. Usually at the bottom of each plate one finds a small text indicating what his sources were. This allows modern researchers to either go back and check what he used, or better, discover an otherwise unknown or forgotten source.

Once when visiting an old militaria collection, its current owner questioned the current author on an odd coat, visibly of 'French Napoleonic infantry' and all bright green with yellow collar and red piping. It did bring up an old memory of a Boisselier plate. Once back home, it was found that it was an Illyrian National Guard junior officer uniform from around 1810–1811 which Boisselier had carefully documented from an auction in the 1930s when this item had been on sale and was bought for that very collection.

Although it is not possible to list all his works, after having spent decades handling Boisselier material, one can classify his production into three main periods. The first one goes roughly from the 1910s to the early 1930s. The drawing and colouring is intricate, often with detailed background and scenery. The use of gouache can be fairly heavy and almost too detailed. Obviously, such art took quite some time to produce. The original plates done for the card series are often close to such quality.

The second period covers the 1930s to the end of the Second World War. This is, in the current author's opinion, the 'best' period. Boisselier's work is precise yet lively. He uses vivid colours combining gouache, watercolour, and ink. The plates featured in this volume correspond exactly to those dates as we shall see.

The third period 1946 to his death is by contrast his worst. Post-war austerity pushed Boisselier to work fast and in volume to make a living. This is when he produced large volumes of plates and his most massive series. They are still quite interesting but are far from as fine as those done previously.

The series presented in this work is a comprehensive and homogeneous one. Each plate is dated in pencil at the back, which is fairly unusual. The plates date from July to December 1943, during the height of the Nazi occupation of France. On one plate next to the date, one can read the name 'Depréaux'. Therefore, it can be deduced that the series was most probably commissioned by Albert Depréaux. He was one of the largest collectors of military documentation in France in the first half of the twentieth century. A regular contributor to the La Sabretache bulletin, he had also been instrumental in the organisation of the military aspects of the pre-war grand colonial exhibition.

Before 1939 he also published a volume on marine and colonial troops as well as one on eighteenth century military uniforms. He was also the original owner of what has become known as the 'Otto manuscript', a series of contemporary gouaches representing the French army in 1807 and which is now part of the very large Anne S.K. Brown Military Collection.

It can be fairly surprising that this series was produced during the dark period of the Nazi occupation. Boisselier was indeed working in German-occupied Paris, and it was hard to procure basic artist's material such as paper, ink, and colours. However, this was the case too for Rousselot who actually started his well-known series of printed plates on the French army at about the same time. How could this be?

Well, it should come as no surprise that during the war, one of the main group of customers for these military artists came from the occupying German army. Many of its officers were passionate militaria collectors. French military artists produced large volumes of artwork for German officers, and one of the side benefits was that they had no shortage of supplies to ensure completing such works, as well as for other projects. After 1944, many such series ended up unsold and could be picked up at low prices with some dealers. Was this precise series part of such commissions? It is difficult to say. The French revolution was not badly looked upon by the German regime as they considered themselves 'patriotic revolutionaries', but it is more probable this was indeed done at the request of Albert Depréaux. Another series featured in the same auction when it was bought covers the personal household of Napoleon III and is also dated from the same period. Such theme is much more a 'French' rather than a 'German' topic of interest.

For his 'French Army of the Revolution' series, Boisselier used multiple contemporary sources, mainly those he could find in large well known public libraries in Paris: the Bibliothèque nationale de France (Hennin collection, Melinet manuscript), and the Bibliothèque des Invalides (Dubois de L'Estang and Vanson collections). He also used contemporary text sources such as the *Journal Militaire*. Overall, Boisselier tried as much as possible to rely on period sources. However, it must be pointed out that despite aiming at being as accurate as possible, some of the plates do not match exactly the original sources. Boisselier sometimes modified the source, correcting what he thought was a mistake or perhaps having wrongly noted some details.

Regardless, if it were not for Boisselier, many such types would not be known and here in a few cases, he truly documents some figures for the first time. This series has never been published in its entirety and is a both a worthy contribution to our knowledge of French Revolutionary armies and a tribute to Boisselier's talent.

2

'Forward, children of the fatherland!' – True Tales of Volunteers

The Volunteer Whose Fame Came with Waterloo

On 6 November 1792, a young volunteer had his first true baptism of fire on the battlefield of Jemmapes in Belgium. Fate would have it that the last time he would later be on a battlefield was some 22 years later, barely some 54 kilometres (33 miles) to the north-east, south of Mont-Saint-Jean, at the battle of Waterloo.

He would acquire on that evening an undying fame, although he always objected to it. Without any doubt, a brash general officer, he would be assumed to have uttered a heroic phrase in an answer to a call to surrender from a British officer: 'The Guard dies and does not surrender!' Given his reputation and according to those who knew him well, what he actually replied was probably but one word, famously to go down in history as 'le mot de Cambronne' (Cambronne's word).

Pierre Cambronne was indeed one of those young men who answered the military call of the revolution quite early. Born in the affluent city of Nantes in December 1770, he was a little over 18 years of age when reformative politics started to hit this rather conservative town. His family had settled there only recently, attracted by business prospects. They had means but were not yet part of the upper layers of Nantes society. He belonged to those young men from the emerging middle class who were educated, yet still on the side lines of power and wealth with few prospects. They eagerly answered the call when the revolution needed them as they saw an opportunity to rise.

After having been one of the first to join the Nantes national guard, Cambronne continued his first military career by transferring, like most of his comrades to the 1er Maine-et-Loire bataillon de volontaires at the end of July 1792. This is how, he had ended up on the field of Jemmapes on 6 November 1792. Like many other volunteers, he went home in early 1793, putting an end to this first experience in the military.

Back in Nantes, he found the situation to be worrying. The Royalist insurrection in the Vendée was threatening the city. The attack on Nantes was the high tide of the 'Great Catholic and Royal Army'. On 28 and 29 June 1793, Royalists tried to take the city, only to be pushed back, demoralized by the loss of their iconic general-in-chief Cathelineau, shot dead during one of the assaults.

In early June Cambronne had enlisted again, this time in a local volunteer formation the légion nantaise. This time, it was for good, and he would not leave the army until after Waterloo.

Cambronne's early career was typical of that of many other local volunteers. He participated actively in the ferocious civil war which was waging in the west. He steadily climbed up the ranks within this 'legion' following its name changes until it finally was incorporated into the 46e demi-brigade. He then fought in all the major actions of the eastern and German theatres of war being present at Zurich and Hohenlinden.

After nine years of warfare, Cambronne had achieved the rank of *capitaine* of the grenadiers in the 46e, which was now posted as part of the army of Boulogne, being readied for the planned invasion of Great Britain.

Cambronne had not been formally trained as an officer, and all he had learnt had been in the field. Still given his good education, he was literate enough to be able to dive into military manuals. An inspection report indicated the following: 'very knowledgeable in both theory and practice. In his hot head he has both honour and hot blood'.[1] The later was quite indicative of his temper, and quite typical of many of these men who had seized their opportunity through obvious physical courage but also brutality and brashness. Cambronne also achieved a reputation as a hard drinker and brawler. The Empire, and the Guard would offer him further advancement, but he was no material for the restored Royalist army of 1814.

Cambronne's personal life followed the image of this rough, unpolished man. He had madly fallen in love in Boulogne with the 24-year-old daughter of a lace merchant. His love interest was no Jane Austen character. She seemed to have had quite some experience with men, especially from the military, and her dealings with Cambronne were fast, and less than platonic. For her he was probably one of several lovers, but not for him, as she was the one and only. He quickly considered marriage, but he knew that his future bride's (all too well known) reputation would probably bar him from his commanding officer's mandatory approval. She, on her side, was far from wishing to leave the merry life she had led up to then and so she repeatedly declined his proposals. Yet, she entertained with him a long correspondence and saw him at intervals when he had a leave. This exchange of letters lasted until well after Waterloo as the last one sent to her by Cambronne can be dated to around 1818.

Cambronne finally settled down in Nantes in 1816 marrying in 1820 a twice widowed well-to-do British woman whose last husband, an American, had bought property in the area. He died in 1842 at the age of 72.

If it had not been for his role at Waterloo, Cambronne would have been forgotten by history. His career was typical of those early Revolutionary volunteers who were lucky to survive the many battles and campaigns of the revolution, and who rose through the ranks through brute force and will.

The Tax Auditor Who Became a Hussar

In June 1792, a dashing 21-year-old lad left his native Jura mountains to become a vérificateur (auditor) with the ferme générale (tax administration) in Paris. Our young clerk had hesitated between the military and this pencil-pushing profession, as surprising as it may seem.

Our young clerk was Nicolas-Philibert Desvernois, who was the son of an accomplished tax official; his brother was already part of that administration and the financial conditions he was being

---

1 Service Historique de la Défense (SHD): box reference XB 437: Inspection report by *général de division* Baraguey d'Hilliers – quoted by Stéphane Calvet in *Cambronne, la légende de Waterloo* (Paris, Vendémiaire, 2016), p.87.

offered were excellent. He had belonged to the Jura Garde nationale as a musician and had attended the fête de la fédération in July 1790. Back in the Jura, waiting for an appointment and not seeing it coming, he had pre-enlisted in the Penthièvre infantry regiment. But when the offer from the tax administration finally had come through just after his pre-enlistment, he opted for the plum appealing life of a young Parisian dandy.

It was therefore with quite some confidence that he had come to Paris. Still eager for the military he joined the Garde nationale section des enfants rouges (Red Children quarter section) as a chasseur.

Desvernois was, unlike many Parisians at the time, not a revolutionary firebrand. In June 1792, he was actually an ardent supporter of the constitutional monarchy. Yet, in June 1792, with revolutionary fever sweeping the country, he quickly realized that this was hardly the time to be a Royalist. Attending the club of his Garde nationale section, he was brutally told that, as a young bachelor, his presence should be with the volunteers at the borders, and that he ought to be leaving his job at the tax administration to married men who had not been called to service. After this first incident, there was another one more violent one in a theatre where he had gone, not knowing it was a favourite hangout for the most extreme revolutionaries, the Jacobins. He openly expressed his distaste, ending with a major brawl.

After the 10 August 1792, the storming of the Tuileries, and the imprisonment of the Royal family, Desvernois realized it was time for him to flee Paris. And so, he joined the Hussards de la liberté and became a hussar.

Fighting first on the Rhine with his unit, Desvernois quickly established himself as courageous and smart, rising to NCO rank by 1793. His unit having become the 7e bis hussars,[2] he was part of the army of Italy under Bonaparte as a *sous lieutenant*. He was always at the forefront, usually chosen for his daring and intelligence. He played a key role at the Battle of Lodi when on a reconnaissance mission he found a ford to enable the French to cross the river and attack the Austrians.

In 1798, Desvernois as part of the 7e bis hussars were part of the expedition to Egypt and his actions, especially his individual duels against Mamelukes became the stuff of legend. Leaving Egypt with the rank of *capitaine* he continued his career into the Empire. Stationed in Italy he transferred to the service of Naples under Murat, commanding the Neapolitan 1e chasseurs à cheval. He resigned as many French officers in 1814 as Murat chose the allied side. Ultimately, having somewhat by chance avoided being in the service of Napoleon both in 1814 and then 1815 (still being in Italy), he maintained his position in the army under the second restoration, retired in 1823 and came back to active service in 1830, only to go on definitive retirement in 1834 and dying in 1859.

Desvernois, unlike Cambronne was not a revolutionary zealot. He was a liberal monarchist and was attracted to the army yet had prospects in the royal tax administration. Events pushed him to the military. Once in the service, he proved himself as ardent as any other Revolutionary volunteer.

The Artist Volunteers

British readers remember of course the famous Artists' Rifles which had a distinguished history throughout both world wars and was created in the mid-nineteenth century with an initial

---

2   In this context, bis means an additional unit of a regiment.

recruitment of artist volunteers. The French revolution had its own version, the *compagnie des arts.*

At the height of the crisis in France created by the foreign invasion and the need for volunteers, a letter was sent to the minister of war on 4 September 1792:

> The citizens of the Louvre section, gathered today as a general assembly in their usual meeting place in the church of Saint-Germain-L'Auxerrois, were quite satisfied to hear the young artists of the school of Paris which has its residence in the Louvre express their wish to form a company of arts and rush on to the borders to defend the state, we have decided… to give to the company of arts students, weapons and clothing which they might need to be fully equipped…we have received the enlistments from about 80 of these artists.[3]

Indeed, according to the memoirs of one of these young men, students in literature, science, law, medicine, and the fine arts had assembled at the Louvre. They had agreed to enlist as a company and had even painted their own banner with a statue of Minerva on it!

The same young man indicated that although barely 17 he was probably the youngest and was overloaded with all what he thought he needed to carry: a helmet made of cardboard with a horse-hair crest, a cartridge box filled with rounds, a 15lb musket, a sabre 'which could have slaughtered Goliath', a cooking pot with a bowl, a knapsack, a sleeping bag, army bread and meat for four days, plus of course a complete volunteer's uniform not to forget the many tears from his beloved mother he also carried away with him in his heart.

No time was wasted before the company suffered its first casualty. On their first night together, which they spent in the Louvre palace, a young painter, either over-excited or under the influence of too much drink, mistook a large window for a door and crashed several floors below onto the palace courtyard, thus putting a brutal end to his military and artistic careers.

Given the fury of the period, a company elected its *capitaine*, a young man who had briefly served in a dragoon regiment, and then the finest looking lad was picked as *lieutenant*. The regiment left Paris a few days later, fully equipped and organized. It bid farewell to the National Convention deputies then assembled in the Tuileries palace, just a few yards away. The president of the legislative session on that day declared 'let your weapons be a rampart for the fatherland and soon your brushes and your writings will tell of your victories.'[4]

And thus, to the music and words of the *Marseillaise*, the company of arts paraded away. Once the sight of Paris vanished from the horizon, they all said 'Now, we're soldiers!'[5]

However, this enthusiasm was soon washed out by heavy rain and hard campaigning. The compagnie des arts ended up doing marches and counter-marches. During the winter of 1792, they were stationed in Sedan. Using their natural artistic talents, they spent their time wooing the peasant girls with music, songs, poetry, and portraits. Never had the locals being used to such intellectual prowess from the military. The enemies were also quite surprised. When they captured men from the company, they would find in their knapsacks neither food nor money to loot but instead leather-bound classics in French or Latin!

---

3   Quoted in Charles-Louis Chassin and Léon Clément Hennet, *Les volontaires nationaux pendant la révolution* (Paris: Quantin, 1902), tome II, p.800.
4   Le Baron Lejeune, *Souvenirs d'un officier de l'Empire* (Paris: unknown publisher, 1851), tome I, pp.16–17.
5   Lejeune, *Souvenirs*, tome I, p.17.

Such happy times were soon over, and the company was called back to Paris to be disbanded. At the time, the revolutionary terror was at its peak and many of these young intellectuals, fearing for their own lives, found refuge, just as Desvernois had done, by enlisting in the regular army. Our young hero did just that. After having been an infantry *sergent*, he found his way, given his intellectual skills, into an artillery company. Later he transferred into the engineer corps and in 1800 became *maréchal* Berthier's aide de camp.

Louis-François Lejeune, future general and baron of the Empire, left his mark not only through his military service under the Consulate and Empire, but even more by his artistic talent that he exercised in between campaigns and after the Napoleonic wars. He was the author of multiple paintings, many documenting battles and campaigns, starting with the revolution which he had himself witnessed.

Lejeune's volunteering and early military career is much less known than his later exploits as Berthier's aide, and even less so as an academic painter who headed up the academy of fine arts in Toulouse. However, his story is typical of what happened to many gifted and ambitious young men who were swept by the winds of the revolution.

Patriots in Petticoats

Saint-Calais was (and still is today) a rather sleepy town in the Loire area, far away from the French borders and therefore quite safe from any foreign invasion. Even as the west was swept by Royalist insurrection, it was still distant enough not to be at risk.

Yet, Saint-Calais in the 1790s eagerly embraced the revolution. It had a growing bourgeois middle-class composed of tradespeople and affluent landowners who saw in it the opportunity to rise above the local and fairly useless nobility. To till the land, it also boasted a large population of agricultural workers bound to the soil and those who owned it. They were of course even more enthusiastic of the changes that were happening.

On 10 March 1793, the directorate of the district of Saint-Calais, its local Revolutionary government, was assembled to enlist volunteers. The King had already been guillotined and the Republic was living its first months with full revolutionary ardour.

On that day, the members of the directorate were then faced with an improbable volunteer, as it was not a he but a she.

According to the documents left by the directorate, she was certainly no beauty pageant contestant nor could lay claim to being the fairest maid on the village green. Marie Savonneau (literally, soapwater) stood a mere 1.54 metres (a little over five feet), with brown hair and eyebrows, yellow-brown eyes, a flat nose, a large mouth, a long, hooked chin, and her face laden with smallpox scars. This was not the first time she was showing up to volunteer as she claimed to have tried for two days to enlist to 'rush to the defence of the fatherland but that the town administration had refused to enlist her because of her sex and that, persistent in her desire to use her arms to uphold liberty and equality, she presents herself to the Directory and prays that they accept her voluntary enlistment.'[6] Faced with such eagerness, the Directorate, which technically was above the town administration, agreed to comply with her wish and that it had to be 'greeted with applause as she sacrifices herself

---

6 Quoted in Léon Deschamps, 'les femmes soldats dans la Sarthe', *La révolution Française: revue d'histoire moderne et contemporaine*, October 1904, pp.327–328.

willingly for the fatherland'.[7] They furthermore justified their decision with the following statement: 'Considering that Marie Savonneau leads a good life of fine morals, that she has had up to now a conduct beyond reproach and that she undertakes male chores every day. Given her looks and obvious muscular build, there seemed to be little risk Marie Savonneau would become a target for her over-sexed male comrades! Marie Savonneau was in all likelihood a farmhand, a robust and strong labourer, little different from the other volunteers she probably worked with in the fields.

Following this decision, two other women came forward to volunteer with the Directorate, on 21 March, Marie Trotté, and 22 March, Magdeleine Manceau. The Directorate was less elaborate in documenting these two other cases.

Marie Savonneau was then sent to the Directorate of the Department of the Sarthe on 16 March 1793, where a former National Assembly deputy, citizen Livré offered to provide her with all the necessary clothing and equipment. Obviously, Marie Savonneau was the first female volunteer from the Sarthe department. We have no proof she was in contact with the other two women which followed in her footsteps, but one can assume that news had travelled fast locally and had led to their own enlistment.

What was Marie Savonneau's later fate? She joined the 1er bataillon de la Meurthe and was engaged in five separate actions. At Coussun, near Maubeuge on the northern border, little Marie was wounded. The National Convention – the Republican government – voted her 300 livres (November 1793) and then a further 500 (April 1794) for her wounds.[8]

On 30 April 1793, the Republican government had enacted a law which specifically excluded from all armies all women who were present with them either serving in the military or as a camp-followers. However, many who were present in units in active duty continued serving until they were either wounded or the law was finally applied by the incumbent commanding officers.

The rationale for such a law was morality. It limited female presence to that of registered washer women, suttleresses, and made sure that any woman of 'loose and bad morals' would be excluded. The presence of women in uniform fighting alongside men was perceived as too strong a carnal temptation.

How many women answered the revolutionary call like Marie Savonneau? It is hard to answer such a question. There are those who left a trace as their presence was well publicized, such was the case for the beautiful Fernig sisters who were quite active in the very early phases of the Revolutionary Wars, following the destruction of their family home by the Austrians. They conducted guerrilla warfare on the northern border, became aides de camp and were considered to be of officer rank. One of the two was even suspected of having had the future King Louis-Philippe as her lover. There was also Thérèse Figueur who left memoirs of her alleged exploits as a dragoon under the revolution and then the Empire.

Other women have left a few traces in the National Convention debates, such was the case for Marie Savonneau, when they were granted financial help or pensions. Local archives also hold, as in the case of Marie Savonneau, many details. Their number was probably not in tens, but probably at least a hundred if not more.

The central French military archives actually hold a series devoted to women soldiers. It groups all such files for the entire eighteenth and nineteenth centuries. Its listing does not indicate which

---

7   Deschamps, 'les femmes soldats dans la Sarthe', p.328.
8   F. Gerbaux, 'les femmes soldats pendant la révolution', *La révolution Française: revue d'histoire moderne et contemporaine*, July 1904, p.55.

period the files relate to (note that the 1870–1871 war saw many cases of female enlistment). A quick survey indicates that there are probably around 15–20 files related to the revolution. One deserves to be narrated as it stands out in terms of volume (over 100 pages) and content, that of Angélique Duchemin.

Angélique Duchemin was the daughter of a soldier in the Limousin regiment. She was born in 1772 in Dinan in northern Britany where the regiment was then stationed. An unofficial (being a girl) regimental child she was already noticed by an NCO who is claimed to have said 'she would make a fine soldier if she were not a woman'.[9] Two of her brothers were, unlike her, registered regimental children.

On 8 June 1785, a 23-year-old lad, André Brulon enlisted in the Limousin regiment and 5 years later as a *caporal* he married Angélique, who had turned 18 years of age. The regiment was now stationed in Ajaccio, Corsica, Bonaparte's birthplace. In 1792, André and Angélique had a daughter, whom they named Andrée.

Corsica had become French in 1768 but had remained quite turbulent, reluctant to be under French rule, under the leadership of its charismatic leader, Pasquale Paoli. Paoli's partisans were fighting for independence. Napoleon's parents sided at some stage with Paoli and even the young Napoleon considered joining that cause. During one of the numerous brawls and skirmishes which plagued the island and the town of Ajaccio, André Brulon was killed, probably in early 1793.

Although this was past the date of 30 April 1793 and the passing of the law forbidding any woman from serving in the army, Angélique pleaded her cause with the local commanding general, Casabianca. She was allowed to replace her husband in the ranks. She quickly rose to the rank of *caporal-fourrier*, as she had obviously received a good enough education. She knew how to read, write, and add up. Having been born in the regiment, she also had a close knowledge of its inner working and the basic military skills, including drill.

At the beginning of 1794 Angélique was in charge of a small garrison in the fort of Gesco close to Calvi. They were then faced with an attack from a mixed force of British regulars and Corsican partisans. Angélique's troops defended themselves and pushed their enemies back. In the process Angélique received a sabre cut to the right arm and a dagger thrust in the left. Running out of ammunition she decided to go and get supplies from Calvi. She crossed the enemy lines and brought back an ammunition convoy led by some 60 women. Later as Calvi was besieged, Angélique again proved her physical courage by leading the fight at the front, having her forage cap shot through with several bullets! Finally, during that siege she was severely wounded by a ball splinter in the left leg and could no longer be on active frontline duty.

Angélique still stayed in the army and became a *commis aux écritures* (accounting clerk) for the army in Italy. She was finally released, on account of the 30 April 1793 law, on 17 November 1797 and admitted to the Invalides in Paris as an invalid veteran.

In Italy, both her father and brothers had died on service and so she found herself, at 25 years of age alone with her five-year-old daughter. Unfortunately, she was expelled from the Invalides in 1798 and sent with a stipend to the Rousselet barracks in Paris. She found the situation there was to be far from ideal and she wrote a letter to the minister pleading for being admitted once again to the Invalides. She felt she and her daughter were in the Rousselet barracks 'exposed to a thousand dangers, and she worried less for her than for her daughter'.

---

9   SHD: file reference 1YI-10: Angélique Duchemin. All quotes relating to Angélique Duchemin are directly sourced from this file and the numerous contemporary documents it contains.

Angélique finally re-entered the Invalides on the 14 December 1798, and was to remain there until her death in 1859!

Given all the above one can easily understand why her file in the French archives is so thick. Yet, Angélique's story does not stop there. Under the Bourbon restoration she petitioned for the légion d'honneur which had been promised to her. She even wrote that her husband had been killed during a rebellion during Easter 1791 led by 'country folks' under Bonaparte's command against the 'town folks'. However, her daughter was baptized in 1792 with her husband attending and therefore he was quite alive!

However, no woman was then (1822) allowed to receive the légion d'honneur. As a compensation, it was decided to grant Angélique the honorary rank of *sous lieutenant* with the relevant financial pension.

Angélique finally received the red ribbon of the légion d'honneur she so richly deserved on 15 August 1851 from the hands of Louis-Napoleon Bonaparte, then the 'Prince President' of the Second Republic, but soon to become Napoleon III. Overall, Angélique had outlived six different political regimes, and of all the women who had fought during the Revolution and Empire, she was one of the bravest.

3

The Plates

As indicated previously each plate was dated by Boisselier on the back, but also numbered on the front. They are presented in the original numbering sequence which has some logic in presenting infantry and artillery then cavalry and services in more or less in chronological order.

Plate 1
Capitaine au 75e regiment d'infanterie, ci-devant Monsieur, 1791–92. Recueil de Marbot. Tambour de Grenadiers 102 régiment d'infanterie, d'après Victor.[1]

The first three plates of the series show French infantry as it entered the war, still wearing its traditional white uniform of royal vintage. It was only on 21 September 1792 that the French monarchy was formally abolished, with the French Republic established on 25 September 1792 in its place.

The fledgling French Republic was at on 20 April 1792, and the army that fought during the first months and achieved victory at Valmy on 20 September 1792 was effectively the old royal army, combined with some of the newly raised 'patriotic' forces.

On 1 October 1786, three years before the revolution, following several previous regulations (1767, 1776, 1779) yet another dress regulation was published. Ever since the Seven Years War (1756–1763), the army had gone through multiple changes in its organisation, tactics and therefore uniforms. The 1786 règlement (regulation) was the culmination of all those efforts. A thick and exhaustive text, much of it was to stay valid until 1812. Even by that late date, this new modern regulation was not fully applied and certainly not to the Imperial Guard. The 1786 text was influential until the end of the Revolutionary and Napoleonic wars.

Although it was quite comprehensive and well thought out, it required multiple adaptations to be put in effect. Accordingly, a number of additional texts were published, adjusting it or giving clarifications on some of its content.

By 1791, it had become obvious that a new complete regulation was needed. A complementary text came out on 1 April 1791, with the very apt title of 'provisional instructions for the clothing of troops' and with as a subtitle 'provisional instruction which will be followed by the regiments in

---

1   Captain from the 75th Infantry Regiment, formerly Monsieur's, 1791–92. Marbot collection. Grenadier Drummer from the 102nd Infantry Regiment, after Victor. Dated July 1943.

the various branches of service, while waiting for the new regulation that his Majesty proposes to give without delay regarding the clothing and equipment of his troops'.

The opening statement read of the new complimentary text stated that 'the regiments in the various branches of service will comply, when it comes to clothing and equipment of men and horses to the prescriptions set in the 1 October 1786 regulation in all matters which are not contrary to the present instruction'.[2] This effectively meant that regimental administrations had to combine both the 1786 regulation and the 1791 instruction to come up with the new required uniform. It is actually probable that some of the changes set forth in this new text had been already implemented by units as they had been found more practical than those featured in the original 1786 text.

Capitaine au 75e regiment d'infanterie
Boisselier indicates as his source for this figure the 'recueil de Marbot'. Indeed plate 70 of volume 3 of Marbot and Noirmont's massive work shows in the background an officer of the 75e quite similar to this one, but with a few variations.

With this type, Boisselier displays the regulation uniform worn on active daily duty by an officer. While the 1 April 1791 instructions did not give specific details for officers, the instructions on infantry service dated 24 June 1792 indicated that officers would usually wear a hat and that the regulation helmet or bearskin would be worn only on active duty (parades, reviews, campaign). It is quite likely that this text simply put in writing what had become common practice within the officer corps.

This *capitaine* therefore wears the 1786 regulation three cornered hat with a small plume white at two-thirds of its base with the regimental colour for a third at its top. Under this plume, but not visible there was a tricolour cockade of red, blue, and white (with red at the centre).

The 1791 regulation had given scarlet as the distinctive colour and 'yellow' buttons to the 75e. This colour was worn at cuffs, lapels and turnbacks, as well as piping to the collar, pockets, and cuff patches. The major design changes to the uniform coat were to add cuff lapels, (something the French army was to keep for decades to come), and remove the three lower buttonholes on the left side under the lapels while keeping the three buttons on the right. Another improvement was to ensure one could easily insert a finger between the collar and the neck of the man. Practically, this meant that the cut of the coat was to be more comfortable!

On 15 January 1792, changes in organisation and the addition of new units created yet another set of instructions and had changed the colour distinctions within the French infantry regiments. According to these the 75e was to have collar and cuff patches all scarlet and change to white buttons.[3] Whether this was actually done is an open question as within the next few months war and the multiple changes in organisation meant that French infantry regiments displayed a bewildering array of uniforms within their ranks.

Royal symbols were still quite visible at this stage: the gilded gorget worn by this officer had the silver royal crest in its centre and the turnbacks bore the traditional French royal lilies braided in gold.

Under the waistcoat, officers would wear a fine shirt with the tip of the cuffs showing slightly at the edge of the sleeves. A white collar was to be worn under the coat at the neck. It was to be black for campaign wear. Hair was to be powdered and worn in a queue which was tied with a black silk ribbon at the back.

---

2   *Instruction provisoire sur l'habillement des troupes au 1er avril 1791*, p.2, author's collection.
3   White buttons were silver or pewter, whereas yellow were gold or brass.

Aside from the gorget, which displayed officer status, ranks were indicated via epaulettes. These were fairly diminutive compared to what they were to become in later years. A *capitaine* would have a full epaulette with tassels on the left shoulder and a simple flat epaulette on the right. These were to be the same the colour as the buttons, in this case gold. A full *capitaine* would have them of solid gold or silver, a *capitaine en second* would have a thread of scarlet silk running through the length of the epaulettes, and a *capitaine remplaçant* would have two such threads.

The 'English style' boots as shown here would remain popular throughout the period until 1815 and beyond.

In case of bad weather, officers were allowed to wear a 'coat' which was actually a large cape with a rotunda. In its initial design in the 1786 regulation it was white, and given how impractical this had proven, the King had quickly allowed it to be of medium blue colour with the collar being of the distinctive colour. The rotunda was edged with a lace of the button colour piped with the distinctive colour.

Finally, officers would officially only have a straight sword as armament. In practice, in the field, they would also carry small flintlock pistols in their back pockets and in some cases a privately purchased fine musket.

The 75e, previously ranked 77e was quite special as it had had as its *colonel propriétaire*, the King's older brother, the count of Provence, Louis-Stanislas (the future Louis XVIII). By tradition, the King's eldest brother was called Monsieur (My Lord) and so his regiment was named régiment de Monsieur (My Lord's regiment). The regiment had scarlet as its distinctive colour as this was Monsieur's colour. The coat buttons had his personal crest. The unit had met its honorary colonel only once in 1771 at Fontainebleau. Monsieur had reviewed his regiment and discussed with the officers wearing its uniform. Provence, as he was also called, had no calling for the military and if this was the first time he saw his personal unit, it was also his last!

A section from the regiment had served as marines during the American War of Independence and had suffered from some casualties in 1782. In 1789, when the revolution in France broke out the regiment was stationed on the eastern border in Metz.

By 1 January 1791, it was based on the southeast Alpine border in Briançon. The new infantry organisation dealt away with the old regimental names and ranked the units by number. This gave the regiment its final ranking as 75e, number which now replaced Monsieur's crest on the buttons.

In 1792, given its location it was made part of the armée du Midi (army of the South) under *lieutenant-général* Montesquiou, but saw no action. In March 1793, it moved north and was part of the Army of the Rhine.

After 1794, it becomes almost impossible to trace what became of the battalions of the old 75e. The regulations passed on 21 February 1793 stated that each old line battalion was to be combined with two volunteer battalions to form a new unit called a demi-brigade de bataille (battle half brigade). Given this, the new 75e was actually made up from the first battalion of the 38e regiment and two volunteer battalions (Vosges #1 and Côte d'Or #17)! What had become of the two battalions of the original 75e? On 3 June 1794, in Wissembourg the new 139e demi-brigade had been formed with the first battalion of the 75e, the Indre et Loire Grenadiers, and the fifth volunteer battalion from Seine-et-Marne. On 29 June 1794, the 140e was formed in Answeiler with the second battalion of the 75e the third volunteer battalion from the Doubs and the 11th from Jura (actually both volunteer battalions came from the very same area near the Swiss border). This was the end of the 75e, formerly Monsieur's regiment. At the same time, the uniform was standardized across all of French infantry displaying the national colours of blue, white and red.

Tambour de Grenadiers 102 régiment d'infanterie
Whereas the captain of the 75e was a perfect representation of the old pre-1789 army, this drummer of the 102e shows the evolution of the royal army.

The 102e was a new unit. It was officially formed on 24 January 1792, but it had been in existence since 6 September 1791. It had been formed from two battalions of the Paris Garde nationale which were paid troops, formerly the first and second battalions of the Gardes Françaises. These had been part of the King's household troops and considered elite. During the revolutionary events of 1789, the Gardes Françaises had squarely sided with the revolutionaries and had actually taken an active part in the storming of the Bastille. They had been rewarded by being taken under the pay of the city of Paris and thus had become the Garde nationale soldée de Paris. The paid Gardes nationale having been disbanded, they were formed into a line infantry unit combined with the first Garde nationale battalion from the Haut-Rhin (Alsace).

After having being stationed in Paris, it joined the armée du centre in July 1792 under Luckner. The 102e was in the thick of the action and was present at the victory of Valmy on 20 September 1792. Its two battalions continued fighting: the first as part of the armée du Nord, the second as part of the armies on the Rhine. On 18 January 1795, the first battalion formed the 179e demi-brigade along with the 6e bataillon de volontaires de Paris and the 7e bataillon de volontaires de l'Oise. On 6 June 1795, the second battalion formed the 180e demi-brigade with the 7e bataillon de volontaires d'Haute-Saône and the 2e bataillon de volontaires de Lot-et-Garonne. Just as with what had happened to the 75e, it was the end of the 102e regiment in its original form.

The addition of several new infantry regiments in the fall of 1791 logically forced a new setup for regimental distinctive colours. As we have seen, this was done on 15 January 1792. The colour assigned to the 102e was dark green and was to be displayed on collar, lapels, cuffs and cuff lapels. The buttons were yellow. This is exactly what is shown by Boisselier.

All drummers were required by 1 April 1791 to wear a blue coat instead of white and laced with the 'King's livery'. The lace livery is dark red edged with white and 'white chains' running along the lace. The combination of the blue, white, and dark red was specific to the King and had been in use with the Gardes Françaises.

The grenadier bearskin worn by the drummer had been suppressed in the 1786 regulation. By 1788, it was re-instated and was clearly again indicated in the 1791 instructions. The headdress was fairly low compared to what it was to become in later years. The front metal plate was usually quite simple with only a grenade. The typical grenadier red plume as shown here could be worn. In some instances, the bearskin seemed to have had a front visor.

The drum used is fairly standard for the period: brass with tricolour wooden circles top and bottom. It is quite likely this drum was used when the man was in the Garde nationale soldée de Paris as this was a very commonplace model in the Garde nationale.

Boisselier states that the source for this gouache is 'Victor'. Actually, one can also spot this very same drummer in the background of plate 92 from Marbot and Noirmont's third volume of plates. This is actually not too surprising as Raffet's son wrote in some notes on his own copies of Victor's sketches that 'Marbot owned many of them and used them for his own work'. So who was this elusive Victor? Raffet's son wrote in his notes that Victor was an old soldier who had done many such small sketches which were to be found in Raffet's and Marbot's collection. Many have found their way into the Dubois de l'Estang collection. This motley assembly of various pieces is now in the reserves of the French Army Museum and is nowadays difficult to gain access to. However, Boisselier like other artists of his time, consulted and used it extensively.

Plate 2
Troupes de ligne 1792–1793
Grenadier au 1er régiment d'infanterie de ligne d'après un document contemporain de Breda
Fusilier au 104e régiment d'infanterie de ligne, d'après un dessin contemporain de Victor.[4]

Perhaps the most striking change and innovation in the 1 April 1791 instructions was the introduction of a new type of infantry headdress, a leather helmet to replace the felt hat.

Indeed the 1786 regulation had given a rather elegant Roman style helmet rather similar to that of the dragoons to the fusiliers of the régiments du Roi and colonel-général. By 1788, other units were trying out, as part of a complete redesign of the army uniforms, a stovepipe style cap or shako with at its base a panther skin band.

All were aware that the existing hat had many significant drawbacks: it offered limited protection against sabre cuts; and foul weather could easily turn it into a ridiculous and shapeless form. Following the wars in America, many light infantry units across Europe had been adopting caps of some kind.

The 1791 helmet was therefore both a consequence of assumed practicality and fashion. The instructions did not describe it in any detail just indicating 'a helmet of felt or varnished leather'.[5] A pattern model was to be sent to each unit to serve as a basis for manufacture.

The model adopted was an obvious copy of the British Tarleton helmet, but with a panther skin band, metal reinforcements on the crown and some form of fur or hair crest.

For decades, the majority of our contemporary sources for this 1791 helmet were not actual surviving pieces but period iconography: Hoffmann's remarkable plates, all kinds of period drawings, and watercolours from Holland or Germany. Although the general aspect was somewhat consistent, there were many variations in details and sometimes even its general aspect. One helmet had survived in Douai and had been represented by many artists. Another one, an officer's model, had found its way in the Brunon collection (and can still be seen in the marvellous l'Emperi museum in Provence). Both of these were somewhat similar. The panther skin band on the officer's helmet was artificial fur, while it was painted oilskin on the Douai rank and file version.

Then a few years ago, a major cache of 1791 helmets turned up in a castle chapel in Germany. They had been stowed away for safe keeping during the Revolutionary Wars. There was no question as to their authenticity. All of a sudden, the 1791 helmet jumped from being one of the scarcest and least well known French military headdress to being a piece which showed up in several collections. These original period items almost all lacked the crest. They all had an oilskin painted panther skin base band. They were also found to be one of the ugliest pieces of equipment anyone had seen in a long time! They did look much better once a fur crest could be restored on them, but still, it was obvious they did not make their wearer look good, nor did they seem to offer adequate protection.

It was also apparent that they were somewhat different in design to the other ones known. This did not come as a total surprise, as in these days of pre-industrial production, mass production of identical items was the exception more than the norm.

---

4   Troops of the line 1792–1793. Grenadier from the 1st Regiment of Line Infantry, based on a contemporary document from Breda. Fusilier from the 104th Regiment of Line Infantry, based on a contemporary drawing by Victor. Dated July 1943.
5   *Instruction provisoire sur l'habillement des troupes au 1er avril 1791*, p.6, author's collection.

Boisselier represented the 1791 helmet (and variants) on multiple plates of this series, all based on contemporary iconography. We now know today that the differences he saw and copied were probable existing variations that units had to make do with.

Grenadier au 1er régiment d'infanterie de ligne
The 1er de ligne, according to the 1 January 1791 organisation was not the old Picardie regiment which held the first rank but actually the former colonel-général. There was some logic in this as this was the regiment of the colonel-général de l'infanterie, in other words the infantry commander-in-chief's regiment. The first 12 regiments had black velvet as their distinctive colour. In the case of the 1er, this was on collar, lapels, turnbacks, cuffs, cuff lapels and as piping to the horizontal pockets. Buttons were yellow. The helmet had, for parade a plume on the left side which was to be white for two-thirds with the one-third tip being the facing colour.

Grenadiers had been given back their bearskins in 1788, but it is quite possible that in many units they were given the 1791 helmet for campaigning. Was the plume for parade red for grenadiers? This is quite possible as such plume was to be worn with the bearskin.

The elite grenadier status is displayed via the scarlet epaulettes. Gaiters used on campaign and for the winter months were black or a very dark grey.

Armament was the regulation 1777 musket and the 1767 pattern short infantry sabre (briquet).

There was a manuscript in the town archives of Breda which shows units from Pichegru's troops in 1793. Richard Knötel used it for his Grosse Uniformenkunde. Plate 7 of volume XVIII displays the various infantry types copied, there is indeed on the far right this grenadier. Several other plates in this series by Boisselier show the other figures copied by Knötel .

Fusilier au 104e régiment d'infanterie de ligne
Boisselier mentions he copied a drawing by Victor, probably from the Dubois de l'Estang collection. This man can also be seen on plate 92 of Marbot & Noirmont's third volume.

The 104e, just like the 102e mentioned in the previous plate were raised from the Garde nationale soldée de Paris and were formerly soldiers from the Gardes Françaises. Three regiments had been formed in such manner: the 102e, 103e and 104e. All three adopted dark green as their distinctive colour. Ironically as part of the King's household the former Gardes Françaises had priority over all other infantry units of the army. As the Garde nationale soldée de Paris they also enjoyed a rather elite status. However, their new regiments were, given their numbers, at the lowest rank in the army list!

This man wears the regulation 1791 uniform. His helmet with a broad brim is one of the multiple variations which can be observed in contemporary iconography. Marbot and Noirmont also give it to the 13e Chasseur battalion on the same plate. The 13e and 14e chasseurs were also made up from the Garde nationale soldée de Paris. Therefore, it is very probable that this specific helmet was common to all of these new units and procured in Paris from the same manufacturer.

Like the 102e, the 104e was engaged in the northern campaigns. The 1793 état militaire indicates that the first battalion was with the armée du Nord and the second in Tirlemont in Belgium.

Plate 3
Grenadier au 67e régiment d'infanterie de ligne (ci-devant Languedoc) 1794 – Recueil de Léo
Sapeur au 82e régiment d'infanterie de ligne (ci-devant Saintonge) 1791 – Dessin original de Victor, collection Dubois de l'Estang.[6]

This is the last plate on the series which displays infantry wearing the old royal white uniforms. It does show that these survived beyond the 1792–1793 changes which imposed blue coats with elements of white and red, so as to show the national colours.

Grenadier au 67e régiment d'infanterie de ligne
The source for this figure comes from a very scarce volume comprising of three coloured plates published in Leipzig in 1794 by Leo. Although of a fairly naïve execution, those plates are quite precise in their details and an excellent contemporary source. The third plate shows two 'line troops grenadiers' which both wear the old white uniform and were, given the date of publication, probably seen in Germany in 1793.

Boisselier has remained rather faithful to the original print. He added a grenade to the bearskin plate which is shown without any ornament on the print. He also drew a sizeable knapsack whereas the original illustration shows a smaller type worn very low on the hip.

The 67e, formerly Languedoc, was posted to Neuf-Brisach in Alsace as part of the army of the Rhine in 1793 under Custine. It participated in some actions around Mainz during the summer and was then transferred to the armée du Nord.

Sapeur au 82e régiment d'infanterie de ligne
The source for this is a drawing by Victor in the Dubois de l'Estang collection. Soldiers equipped with tools were first introduced in infantry regiments as early as 1710. In 1766, it was decided to have two carpenter-soldiers per company and the 1767 regulation gave them a leather apron, a bearskin, a sabre-saw and an axe. They were however to be put in service only during times of war. In the 1770s, they were no longer mentioned, but came back formally in 1780 as a regular part of the companies. The 1786 dress regulation also abolished the wearing of a bearskin but this returned in 1788 just as it did for the grenadiers.

Victor's drawing which inspired Boisselier is assumed to have been done by an eyewitness. The general aspect of this sapper would last all through the Revolutionary Wars and indeed into the Empire, except for the dropping plume.

The bearskin plate has as its ornament a typical revolutionary design: the Roman lictor's staff with a Phrygian bonnet, the whole circled with laurel wreaths.

Sappers were typically strong and massive men who wielded a heavy carpenter's axe and bore a special sabre which doubled up as a saw thanks to the saw-tooth design of the back of the blade. If both of these could be used as weapons, they were of little help at some distance. Later, sappers were to be officially armed with small muskets, but at this time they did not carry firearms officially. In practice, they were often, as shown here armed with two small pistols which they carried

---

6   Grenadier from the 67th Regiment of Line Infantry (formerly Languedoc) 1794 – Léo Collection. Sapper from the 82nd Regiment of Line Infantry (formerly Saintonge) 1791 – Original drawing by Victor, Dubois de l'Estang collection. Dated June 1943.

in holsters in a specially designed belt. They were most probably gendarmerie 1777 short pistols which were also much in favour with officers given their small size.

By 1793, the 82e had its first battalion locked up in Mainz, while the second was in Landau. So, the entire unit was with the army of the Rhine.

Plate 4
Tambour de grenadiers demi-brigade d'infanterie de ligne 1795–1800, d'après un dessin original de Raffet
Grenadier des demi-brigades de ligne 1795–1800, d'après un mannequin du musée de l'armée.[7]

We are leaving behind the old royal army, and this plate shows the ideal depiction of the French Revolutionary infantryman.

On 21, 23, 24 and 25 February 1793, the Revolutionary government enacted a series of decrees which re-organised the entire army.[8] The Convention had to face the threat of invading armies and possible internal counter-revolutionary movements. The decisions were aimed at sorting out the confusion and animosity which reigned within the army while also providing an influx of fresh new recruits.

In its first article dealing with the infantry, it enacted that 'there will no longer be any distinction nor difference in treatment between infantry units called line regiments and the national volunteers'. To that effect, in the second article, the 'infantry of the republic' was to be formed as demi-brigades each combining one battalion from one of the former line infantry regiments and two of volunteers. This was the first 'amalgame' (a term best translated in English as fusion or consolidation). In so doing, the Convention hoped to combine the best of both worlds: the revolutionary fervour of the volunteers and the experience and professionalism of the veteran soldiers of the old royal army. In the next sentence of that second article it was written that 'the uniform will be the same for all of the infantry. It will bear the national colours and this change will happen as and when the administration has to renew clothing. Each demi-brigade will be distinguished by a number on the buttons and on the flags.'[9]

Indeed, the complete change took some time and elements of the old royal uniform were still worn months afterwards. The blue coats of the volunteers, which had now become the norm, often neighboured the old white. This was far from being the most critical concern when it came to clothing as we shall see.

By late 1794 or 1795, one could say that the uniform changes had been completed. The blue coat with white lapels, red collar, cuffs and pipings was to become the almost universal dress of the French line infantryman and was to remain as such, in terms of colours, until 1815.

Boisselier has therefore quite aptly dated both his grenadier drummer and grenadier to a 1795–1800 time span. Both are however not taken from contemporary iconographic sources. They are both reconstructions but each using a different source type.

---

7   Grenadier drummer of a line infantry demi-brigade 1795–1800, after an original drawing by Raffet. Grenadier of a line demi-brigade 1795–1800, after a mannequin in the Musée de l'Armée. Dated August 1943.
8   'Décrets généraux, sur l'Armée', des 21, 23, 24 et 25 février 1793, published in *Le Journal Militaire*, no.9, 3 March 1793, from p.137.
9   'Décrets généraux, sur l'Armée', Article II, p.139.

Tambour de grenadiers demi-brigade d'infanterie de ligne 1795–1800
Boisselier gives as his source 'an original drawing by Raffet'. Auguste Raffet, one of the most gifted and distinguished military artists of the nineteenth century, was born in 1804. Along with Charlet and Bellangé he was quite active in propagating the Revolutionary and Napoleonic legends through his works. Unlike Charlet, who at least was old enough to not only witness at least the imperial period but even be an active military participant in its ultimate stages, Raffet was only 11 years old in 1815! He did interact with veterans, collected uniforms and equipment, and had access to numerous primary iconographies. The grenadier drummer shown here is quite plausible. He displays the national colours via his coat which could still be worn under the Empire, although its cut is probably quite loose and in line with the 1786 regulation cut. His drummer status is distinguished via the red edged with white swallow's nests on his shoulders and with tricolour horizontal laces on his sleeves. Swallow's nests were common for drummers in the royal army, and this fashion was kept and still in use under the Empire. Various kinds of tricolour lace seem to have been adopted, replacing the old royal lace which was dark crimson and white. Grenadier companies were quite proud of their distinctive bearskin headdress. This rather short one is very much of the same kind adopted again in 1791. It has a brass plate decorated with a simple embossed grenade. Typically, bearskins could have cords, tassels, and plume – all scarlet, a colour which was distinctive for the elite grenadier companies. Usually both bearskin and its decorations were worn for full dress, which may be the case here. On campaign and in the field, grenadiers would rather don a simpler three-cornered hat with some form of red plume or pompom. As the man is wearing dark gaiters one can assume he is in the autumn or winter period of the year. He would have white gaiters in spring and summer.

Grenadier des demi-brigades de ligne 1795–1800
If the drummer is taken from a drawing, its companion, a simple grenadier is copied from a mannequin which was on display at the army museum in Paris. Indeed, from the date of the opening of the museum in 1905 to its latest massive renovation a century later, such a figure was exhibited. A black and white postcard shows the original figure but also a much more adequate colour one published in the 1970s by the museum. It shows exactly this uniform with some small differences: dark grey gaiters and a more classic white waistcoat rather than the one shown here with two vertical button rows. When the museum closed down for renovation it did an analysis of the items it had been showing for decades. It was discovered that many were not original but rather later and of a similar pattern or plain modern copies. It is possible that this explains why the mannequin is no longer on display. It did however cut an impressive figure reproducing the ideal image of the Revolutionary grenadier. The scarlet carrot shaped tuft on the bicorn is one of many such variations which were in use by grenadiers.

Plate 5
Fusilier des 1/2 brigade de batailles vers 1796
Officier des 1/2 brigade de batailles vers 1796
D'après une estampe allemande du temps collection Hennin, bibliothèque nationale, cabinet des estampes.[10]

If the previous plate showed us the ideal, perfect Revolutionary soldier, this one brings us back to reality and shows the lack of uniformity and even shoddiness of the French soldier on campaign during the Revolutionary period. Boisselier indicates his source as being 'a German contemporary print form the Hennin collection in the prints department of the French national library'.

The Hennin collection, thus named after its previous owner, Charles Hennin who bequeathed it to the library in 1863 is a massive compilation of thousands of prints related to French history. It boasts some well-known works but also very obscure ones which Hennin collected quite easily back in the mid-nineteenth century.

In this case, the source print is titled 'Ansichten der durch Schwaben im Monath Junii 1796 marschirden Neufrancken' (a view of the new French who marched through Swabia in the month of June 1796). It is indeed a remarkable printed and hand coloured document that Boisselier used for this plate and others. Unfortunately, although the general look and feel are well reproduced, there are numerous differences with the original which need to be highlighted.

Part of the success of the French armies, during the revolution and after was that they did not drag along massive supplies and baggage, unlike their adversaries. The French soldiers very much lived off the land with variable results. This did however ensure they moved faster and more aggressively than their opponents.

Contemporary iconographic testimonials in Holland, Germany and Italy all show French troops remarkably alike: poorly dressed, often in rags with a clear lack of uniformity. After all it was on 27 March 1796 that the newly appointed commander in chief of the army of Italy, Bonaparte told his assembled men:

> Soldiers, you are naked, badly fed, the government owes you much. It can give you nothing. Your patience, the courage you displayed amid those rocks are admirable, but they bring you no glory, no light shines upon you. I wish to lead you on to the most fertile plains in the world. Rich provinces, large cities will be yours, there you will find honour, glory and wealth. Soldiers of Italy, do you lack courage or will?[11]

Fusilier des 1/2 brigade de batailles vers 1796
The term 'de bataille' (battle) or 'ligne' (line) was equivalent and one finds either in contemporary texts, although 'de bataille' seems to have become gradually more common and stayed in use until the demi-brigades became regiments again.

This man is a fusilier and therefore should not carry a short sabre and have only one shoulder belt (which is the case) on which hangs a cartridge box and bayonet. He does however have a sabre. In

---

10   Fusilier of a battle demi-brigade circa 1796. Officer of a battle demi-brigade circa 1796. Based on a German print from the Hennin collection, National Library, print room. Dated December 1943.
11   Proclamation du général en chef à l'ouverture de la campagne, in H. Plon, & J. Dumaine (eds), *Correspondance de Napoléon 1er* (Paris: Imprimeur de l'Empereur, 1865), vol.1, letter 91, p.107.

the original print, this weapon has no hilt and looks to be a captured sapper hanger of German or Austrian origin. He has a tricolour coat similar to the one worn by the grenadier drummer on the previous plate. However, this is absolutely not the case in the original print. On it, this man instead wears and old dark-blue piped white short coat typical of light infantry. In fact, Boisselier for whatever reason transferred this man from light to line infantry! Boisselier has also given him a purple waistcoat which is just plain dark blue in the print. Although he has been observed in 1796, he was still by then wearing the 1791 pattern helmet. This is actually not too surprising as even as late as 1798 there were still some in store which were sent on to Egypt along with Bonaparte's expedition! In the original print, the man looks even more in rags. His trousers, probably made of some captured bed sheets or household cloth, are too short and visibly hastily made up into suitable legwear. His left shoe has its front half cut off and to protect his toes the man has put on some white cloth. He does have a pale blue sock on his right foot. Like in Boisselier's image he does carry a piece of white cloth tied on his shoulder belt and some form of scarf, but of purple colour. He has stuck a loaf of bread on his bayonet and smokes a brown clay pipe. Despite the numerous differences, Boisselier's work is not improbable, but it would indeed have been better if he had stuck to the original.

Officier des 1/2 brigade de batailles vers 1796
This figure is closer to what can be observed on the original print, although there are again differences. The most striking aspect is that this officer carried a backpack typical of the rank and file and not officers. However, given the lack of available transport, many junior officers had no other option and thus had some form of pack to carry their personal items. In the original print the straps and the belt are just slightly darker than the usual belt white, but visibly not of brown leather like shown by Boisselier. The coat worn over his uniform is shown in the print to be medium blue with a red turned-down collar giving it a more military appearance, while Boisselier has chosen to make it more civilian. Another noticeable difference is that the man carries only one pistol and not two. Indeed, officers usually carried two pistols which may explain why Boisselier made such change. They would usually have them in their coat tail pockets as they often adopted small weapons like the gendarmerie regulation pistol. Here the weapon shown is too big to be carried in a coat pocket and has been stuck in the waistbelt. The officer wears a three-cornered hat with a short red plume which seems to indicate he is an officer from a grenadier company. He has tight fitting dark blue breeches buttoning down on the sides. The only real insignia of rank he has is his gorget, which is actually totally plain brass on the original print.

Plate 6
Musicien à la 32e 1/2 brigade de bataille vers 1796 collection Boersch
Musicien à la 57e 1/2 brigade de bataille 1798. Correspondance du Général Victor Perrin au conseil d'administration.[12]

This plate is the only one in the entire series showing musicians and it gives us the opportunity to discuss music and musicians in the French military at the close of the eighteenth century during the

---

12   Musician with the 32nd battle demi-brigade circa 1796. Boersch collection. Musician with the 57th battle demi-brigade 1798. Correspondence from General Victor Perrin to the Administration Board. Dated December 1943.

Revolutionary period. It is first important to clarify that when considering musicians, this excludes drummers and fifers. These were not part of the band but part of their respective companies and had a military status, unlike musicians. Drummers and fifers could be all grouped together for a parade and a review under the leadership of the *tambour-major*, but they were independent from the music band.

Musicians were actually not true military as they did not enlist as the other men would do in a unit. Instead, they were music professionals who signed a contract with an employer that was the military unit, just as it could have been a wealthy individual, or an opera house. The official administrative term used was *musician gagiste* which meant a musician who received 'gages' – payments for a service. To be very precise, the actual contracting body was the administrative council of the unit, composed of representatives of the officer corps.

At the close of the monarchy, infantry units had been authorized to have bands composed of eight musicians. In effect though, regiments could have larger bands or alternatively hire top-notch artists, supply them with the finest instruments, and dress them with extravagance. It all depended on how deep the pockets of the officer corps of that regiment were.

This also meant that musicians could break their contract and leave for another unit where they would receive better pay, or better working conditions. Furthermore, in a world where music was very much appreciated but not so easily accessible, those very same military musicians could be sought out by the local theatres, operas, or the wealthy for private performances.

By reputation, the best musicians were considered to be men from the German lands, and often they would start their career in regiments posted in the east. Gradually their reputation could bring them to positions in Versailles with the Gardes Françaises or Gardes Suisses. Such was the case of the Gebauer family. The father being from Saxony, some of his sons achieved prominence with the Gardes Françaises. When that regiment was disbanded after July 1789, the band formed both the core of the band of the Garde nationale de Paris but also a music school which is the direct ancestor of present-day Conservatoire national supérieur de musique et de danse de Paris, the top music school in France. The Gebauer brothers were later to have a distinguished career throughout the period as composers and musicians for and with Napoleon's Imperial Guard.

Apart from such exceptional cases, the run-of-the-mill French military musician was often a young boy or man who had displayed musical aptitudes as a choir boy in his local church. He would have learned to play basic wind instruments. The odd-looking serpent, so typical of military bands of the period, was originally a church instrument providing a deep sound well suited to liturgy. The most common instrument was the clarinet, and the band master was often the lead clarinet player. Instruments were often of poor quality and, along with other military equipment, would suffer from campaigning. The two well-known memoirs that have come down to us from musicians both mention that their respective clarinets had been fixed with handmade lead keys while on campaign.

The late eighteenth century was of course a period ripe with superb composers. Haydn was the most prominent, especially as he had written music specifically for the military, but tunes by Mozart were also adapted. To these well-known artists, one must add those which have somewhat been forgotten today by the larger public, but which were quite famous then: Grétry, Méhul, Gossec, amongst others. Some of the tunes played by military bands were copied from some of these men's best-known works. Probably the most famous example is Grétry's *la Victoire est à nous* (Victory is ours). A tune taken from a very short scene in one of his pre-1789 operas. These catchy few bars of music were soon to be played and heard as a sign that 'la Victoire est à nous'. The very same Grétry was rather ironically also responsible for what was one of the first truly Royalist anthems. When

Louis XVI took refuge in the Tuileries on 10 August 1792, as he passed between the two rows of noblemen protecting him with drawn swords, they sang 'Ô Richard, Ô mon Roi' (Oh Richard, Oh my King!) another catchy song taken from Grétry's hit Opera *Richard Cœur de Lion*.

Specific songs, tunes, and marches were also written. Many were commissioned by the various Revolutionary governments, but such productions rarely caught on popular fervour. The two most popular tunes *Ça ira!* and *La Carmagnole* were for the first a dancing tune quite popular before 1789, including with the queen who used to play it on her harpsicord, and for the second possibly a song from Piedmont in Italy which had arrived via Marseilles. Both were quite popular during the Revolutionary period and a symbol of French revolutionaries to the point that the Sanfedisti counter-revolutionaries in Naples in 1799 mentioned the *Ça ira* in their own marching and battle song.

Musicien à la 32e 1/2 brigade de bataille vers 1796
Musicien à la 57e 1/2 brigade de bataille 1798

Both of these musicians are from the later period of the revolution. We do know that bands did exist in the early stages of the Revolutionary Wars. In fact, Girault's memoirs indicate that he was present at Valmy, where his band was ordered to play the *Ça ira* by the future king Louis-Philippe while under significant cannon fire. However, iconographic depictions of these are unfortunately scarce.

The 1786 regulation had quite plainly laid down the regulation for the clothing of drummers and musicians. For drummers, the coat colour was to be blue with the King's livery (lace), except for some regiments: the queen's, royal family princes', foreign regiments and those with a *colonel-propriétaire*. These were to wear the specific livery of their *colonel*, which in this case meant a specific coat colour and lace. Musicians were to have a similar coat but with no livery. The cuffs had instead a fine silver lace.

This was however not sufficient enough for officers who wished to display the finest band they could finance and so fashion gradually came in to play. The cuff lace was typically extended to the collar, sometimes edging the lapels. As a distinction, musicians also started having specific epaulettes ending in the three-pointed loop known as trèfle (clover). The silver lace gave way to a lace matching the colour of the coat button, quite often yellow or gold. Finally, when conditions became more affluent regiments started dressing their bands (and drummers) in colours that contrasted with those worn by the rest of the regiment.

The bassoon player on the left has been copied by Boisselier from a series of Alsatian paper soldiers by Boersch. As Boersch probably used the documentation left by his uncle Benjamin Zix, an official artist with the army, who had seen those men, this is a reliable representation. This man wears the same dress as the rest of his unit except for the yellow lace at the cuffs, cuff lapels, lapels and his trèfle epaulettes. The tricolour plume on his hat indicates he belongs to the regimental staff which was indeed the case for the band.

The man on the right belong to the 57e demi-brigade which was commanded at the time by the future *maréchal* Victor (known then as Victor Perrin). In his correspondence with the administrative council of the unit he stipulated what the band should wear: an inverted colours coat, red with blue collar, cuffs, lapels, with gold lace at the cuffs and collar. One will note that the epaulettes are standard and that the man has short black leather boots. Just like for this counterpart in the 32e he has a tricolour plume on his hat. Boisselier gave him a short horn or trumpet as an instrument. Although a gifted artist, Boisselier was not a prime specialist in antique instruments and his rendering of such an instrument is actually quite poor.

Plate 7

Chasseur à la 14e 1/2 brigade légère an VI armée des Grisons
Tambour-Major 18e 1/2 brigade de ligne, an VI, armée des Grisons
D'après des aquarelles de l'époque du citoyen François Muller. Collection Hennin, cabinet des estampes, bibliothèque nationale.[13]

This plate requires first a background explanation on its sources which have been clearly indicated by Boisselier as coming from watercolours by citizen François Muller located in the Hennin collection as part of the massive prints collection of the Bibliothèque nationale de France.

There are indeed two watercolours which have been labelled by their author as having been done by 'citoyen François Muller de Fribourg'. One depicts the attack on Laupen by *général de division* Brune on the 5 March 1798, and the second one, the Battle of Fraubrun on the next day, 6 March 1798. Although the figures are quite small, they are highly detailed and Boisselier could indeed use them as sources for these two figures. Furthermore, there are numerous examples of contemporary iconography in the national Swiss museum in Zurich which shows the same types and actually confirms them.

Chasseur à la 14e 1/2 brigade légère an VI armée des Grisons
The chasseur of the 14e légère does look like a fairly odd figure wearing a short tailed brown coat faced with sky blue. We have ample sources which confirm such oddity, and the 14e légère has often been represented by modern artists such as Ganier-Tanconville (in *Le Passepoil*) and Albert Rigondaud – Rigo – (*Le Plumet* plates – series U, number 8).

We are also lucky in that the 14e légère had in its ranks an officer, Auguste Biggaré who later had a distinguished career under the Empire raising himself to become aide de camp to King Joseph in Naples and Spain, and who wrote his memoirs in 1830. This text, some 30 years after the facts was the occasion for him, as all too often with Napoleonic veterans, to cast himself in a very favourable light, especially when it came to narrating some details of his good fortunes with the local women. Yet, it remains a valuable document explaining how the 14e légère came to being.

It was initially raised after the Quiberon expedition as the Première légion des francs de l'Ouest (the first legion of the Franks) as part of the invading forces to Ireland under *général de brigade* Humbert. Biggaré stated in his memoirs that the officers were rigorously selected, so as to form an elite corps. This may have been true for the officers but was not the case for the men, which mostly came from the ranks of the former royalists who had been defeated.

This first attempt at an invasion of Ireland ended in a semi-disaster given very poor weather conditions. Having failed to land, the legion ended up having to fight on board the ship that was carrying it against two British frigates. Stranded offshore and unable to move, the ship had to wait for two days until a rescue party showed up. Out of the 600 men of the initial legion, between those who died at sea and the greater majority who had deserted, the unit had lost some 500! Reinforced with new recruits, it was then sent to the armée de Sambre et Meuse where it fought on the Rhine. On 1 January 1798, the legion was reorganised and made into a regular unit under the rank of 14e demi-brigade légère. It was then selected to participate in the armée d'Helvétie which was to come

---

13   Chasseur of the 14th light demi-brigade, year 6, Army of the Grisons. Drum-Major 18th line demi-brigade, year 6, Army of the Grisons. From contemporary watercolours by citizen François Muller. Hennin Collection, print room, National Library. Dated October 1943.

to the aid of the pro-French Swiss cantons against the rest of the Swiss confederation and later against the Austrians and Russians. In early March 1798, it was part of the forces that drove on to Bern, fighting at Fraubrunnen, which are the events depicted by François Muller in his work.

Organised as a 'legion', and therefore as a light infantry unit, it was to have typical 'light infantry' uniform features: a short coat with pointed cuffs and pointed lapels, short gaiters, and tight fitting breeches. Biggaré in his memoirs indicated that when it was first uniformed in Saint-Malo it received captured British red coats which had been taken at Quiberon and which had been dipped into blue dye. This had resulted in them having a dark brown almost black colour. This resulted in the legion being called the légion noire (the black legion). To brighten up this rather gloomy outfit, it was decided to give them sky blue collars, cuffs, and piping, as well as hussar-style breeches. Carabiniers had red plumes and epaulettes, chasseurs had green. The original short coats were of the British-Austrian pattern, but as can be seen in Muller's watercolour, as well as in two other period iconographs which are in Zurich, it ended up wearing a regular French light infantry coat. One of the Zurich images shows lapels as sky blue, while the other shows red piping along the breeches. It is quite possible that, as the unit refitted itself some variances in dress pattern occurred. It however remained true to its original dark-brown uniform even as a regular light infantry unit. It was only when it was brought back to France in July 1799 that the men of the regiment received the regulation dark blue uniform.

Tambour-Major 18e 1/2 brigade de ligne, an VI, armée des Grisons
The other figure is a *tambour-major* taken from the other watercolour which shows the attack on Laupen. Although a very diminutive figure it is detailed enough to enable such a fine depiction by Boisselier. As the image also shows the demi-brigade flag as a horizontal blue (at the top) white and red with a large white 18 on an green ground surrounded with gold laurels, it allows us to attribute this *tambour-major* to the 18e ligne.

The man has a regular infantry coat with no indication of any rank and has grenadier epaulettes which may indeed mean he is a rank-and-file grenadier cast in as a *tambour-major*. The only distinguishing feature of his status, apart from his cane is the gold lace on the lapels and buttonholes. The scarlet waistcoat is also worn by two of the drummers on the original image, so this is not specific to the *tambour-major*. The tricolour plume indicates he belonged to the unit's staff. Interestingly, there is another image in Zurich's National Museum which shows a *tambour-major* wearing almost the same type of coat with gold lace on the lapels and buttons, but also on the cuffs. This one also sports gold tréfle epaulettes.

Oddly enough for both figures, Boisselier gave them powdered hair, whereas in both images, the men wear their hair long tied in queues but unpowdered.

Plate 8
Infanterie légère
Carabinier circa 1794 d'après Victor, collection Dubois de l'Estang
Chasseur circa 1793, d'après A. de Marbot et les dessins de Raffet, bibliothèque nationale.[14]

On 21 February 1793, the 14 chasseur battalions and various light volunteer units were reorganised to form the demi-brigades d'infanterie légère, just as at the same time a parallel move was made with the line infantry and volunteers. This was actually achieved by January 1794, forming 22 demi-brigades.

As the line infantry adopted blue coats with white lapels, red collar and cuffs – showing off the three national colours, the light infantry also took on the new main national colour of 'national blue', but true to its tradition of a dark overall dress, it used it for all items of dress: coat, waistcoat, and breeches with the exception of the collar which was to be red. It also adopted two specific 'light' features copied from the light cavalry: cuffs and lapels became pointed. The button colour became white and to brighten up the sombre looking coat, white piping was placed on lapels, cuffs, turnbacks, and pockets. The headdress remained initially the same: the 1791 model helmet and bearskin cap, but on 7 September 1793, it was decreed that the helmet should now be green.

Carabinier circa 1794
This carabinier is copied from a drawing by Victor as part of the Dubois de l'Estang collection and depicts a contemporary soldier. This type was copied by many modern artists, but similar looking figures can be observed in both Revolutionary iconography and somewhat later productions by Charlet, Raffet and others.

His coat is strictly regulation, but his waistcoat has white piping, and his breeches feature white Hungarian knots in imitation of what light cavalry wore. The most distinguishing feature is his headdress which is neither the regulation hat nor a bearskin but a hussar-style mirliton cap with red flame and hanging plume. Such caps seemed to have become popular with the light infantry. Chasseurs would have the same but with green flame and plume. He wears the usual short gaiters imitating light cavalry boots with red lace and tassels.

Chasseur circa 1793
The chasseur is copied from a Marbot plate. He wears the regulation outfit with the exception of piping on his waistcoat and the adoption of green epaulettes which again were gradually becoming a regular chasseur feature. His gaiters are light coloured, probably off white and worn during summer months with green lace and tassel. The most striking part is of course the exuberant helmet which Marbot clearly showed. In the Bibliothèque nationale de France, there are several volumes of sketches done by Raffet's son which show a variety of such helmets and were drawn based on surviving items. These helmets were made to follow the September 1793 decision to have green helmets for the light infantry. In a few cases, they were just green 1791 model helmets, but there were some rather extraordinary models made, usually featuring intricate white metal ornaments. However, they do not seem to have lasted very long and few if any contemporary iconography shows them. None seem to have survived to this day.

---

14 Light infantry. Carabinier circa 1794 after Victor, Dubois de l'Estang collection. Chasseur circa 1793, after A. de Marbot and drawings by Raffet, French National Library. Dated August 1943.

Plate 9
Aérostier et Cannonier à pied 1793
d'après la collection Dubois de l'Estang, dessin de Victor, la collection Boersch etc. Recueil de Lienhart et Humbert.[15]

In the late eighteenth century, Europe experienced an unprecedented wave of scientific and technological innovations due to the combination of intellectual and material means. France was at the forefront thanks to a generation of brilliant scientists and intellectuals. Most of them had lobbied for political and social changes prior to 1789 and so wholeheartedly embraced the revolution.

One of the most exciting technologies which appeared just prior to 1789 was flight. It fulfilled a long-held human dream of at least being able to ascend into the air. In 1783, the first balloon ascent was achieved in Versailles under the watchful and interested eyes of the King and his court. A little over 10 years later, with war now waging, the Revolutionary government constituted a 'proofing committee' on 22 March 1794 which had as its main task to find military applications for new technologies. It was composed of the most brilliant scientists whose names are still familiar to science students today: for example, Monge, Berthollet, Carnot, and Lavoisier. Tests of hot air balloons had been made out of the Tuileries gardens in November 1793, and they had proved conclusive. With support from the proofing committee, experiments and building of a military 'aérostat' (balloon) had been commissioned under the direction of Coutelle and Conté. This balloon called l'entreprenant (the enterprising) achieved several successful ascents on 29 March 1794 in front of the commission. Within the next few days the Committee of Public Safety decided to create a military balloon unit. On 2 April 1794, it issued an order which established a compagnie d'aérostatiers which was comprised of a *capitaine*, a *sergent-major*, a *sergent* and 20 men. It was based just outside of Paris, in the southwest suburb of Meudon. Half of the men were to be craftsmen skilled in masonry, carpentry, painting, and chemistry. Coutelle was appointed as its *capitaine*. Very quickly the unit increased in size to 30 men, with the addition of a *premier lieutenant* and *second lieutenant*.

Its first military deployment came two months later in front of Maubeuge in northern France. Its use was of course to observe enemy movements and report them. On that first day, it seemed its main achievement was to boost French morale and depress that of the Austrians who were wondering what this 'ball' was all about! On 26 June 1794, at the Battle of Fleurus, the balloon stayed up in the air the entire day, transmitting information through a variety of signals and helped in achieving the victory. Although the l'entreprenant did suffer an accident in the weeks that followed it was quickly repaired and a second balloon was built – le martial (the martial). By the end of 1794, the company had become a battalion with two companies each of 30 men and eight balloons were being built. Although they had proven useful, the balloons were also cumbersome to use. Transporting and then setting them up was complex. With warfare being increasingly mobile, they were just not fully up to the task unless used for static situations such as sieges. Although Bonaparte had agreed to bring one along with his army into Egypt, the balloon and its equipment was lost during the Battle of the Nile. However, the aerostatiers company which had accompanied the army to Egypt under the leadership of the brilliant Conté proved incredibly useful as it transformed itself into a military workshop capable of producing and repairing just about anything that was needed.

---

15 Balloonist and foot gunner, 1793. After the Dubois de l'Estang collection, drawing by Victor, Boersch collection etc. Lienhart and Humbert collection. Dated August 1943.

Meanwhile back in France, the École d'aérostatiers de Meudon was abolished on 28 January 1799. Once Bonaparte returned from Egypt and had seized power in late 1799, although he had much appreciated the aerostatiers' support, he did not reverse the decision. Once the last aerostatiers came back from Egypt in 1801, they were transferred to the engineers. Actual instruction on balloons continued as part of the training of military engineers, but no practical use was made until 1870.

Although it was an independent body, the aerostatiers wore uniforms which were inspired by both artillery and engineers adopting especially black as a distinctive colour, from the engineers.

Artillery under the monarchy did not truly exist as an independent branch of service. It was listed like a regiment along with the infantry in the états militaires and ranked as 64th. The entire corps of artillery was composed of seven regiments under the term corps royal de l'artillerie. Each regiment like the infantry had a name. When looking up the regiment de la Fère, garrisoned in Auxonne in the 1790 état militaire, one can find a *lieutenant en second* called de Buonaparté. In itself a quite interesting spelling which gives a clear indication on how the young Bonaparte pronounced his own name with an obvious strong Corsican accent. As with the rest of the army, in 1791, regimental names were dropped. As the war progressed, regiments remained only as administrative bodies and from a practical standpoint, artillery was dispersed as companies attached to the various armies in the field.

As artillery was listed as part of the infantry, its uniform was strictly that of the infantry but with its specific colours.

Aérostier et Cannonier à pied 1793
Both of these figures are stated by Boisselier as having multiple sources: the Dubois de l'Estang collection, Victor's drawing, the Boersch paper soldiers, and Lienhart and Humbert. The latter is a late nineteenth century encyclopaedia on French uniforms itself based on multiple sources including the previous ones mentioned. Note that Boisselier spells 'aérostier', which is a more modern spelling, whereas the correct period spelling is 'aérostatier'.

In its order instituting the balloon companies, the Committee of Public Safety had decreed that 'its uniform shall be: coat, waistcoat and breeches, blue, red piping, collar, cuffs, black, infantry buttons and fatigue pants and waistcoat in blue kersey. The armament of the said company to be of a short sabre and two pistols.'[16]

No indications were given as to possible epaulettes, hat or other elements. Obviously the balloon men were to copy what was worn by the artillery and engineers and the few quasi-contemporary sources we have confirm that. Engineer sappers typically wore red epaulettes as a symbol of their elite status and that may have been the case here too. Likewise white waistcoats seem to have been worn. These are both options chosen by Boisselier. He has not represented the two regulation pistols, and which then would have implied wearing a waist belt.

The artilleryman has often been depicted and is well known. As per the 1786 regulation he wore an overall blue uniform with red piping and scarlet-red cuffs. In 1791 when cuff lapels were adopted these were to be blue with red piping. However, as often with cuff lapels during this troubled period, variations existed, and so scarlet cuffs lapels as shown here by Boisselier were also to be found. By regulation, artillerymen did not have the standard infantry sabre but actually a specific Roman style one with a straight double-edged blade and the pommel ending with an eagle head. Quite often, other styles were supplied. Here Boisselier is showing a typical Revolutionary sabre with an intricate basket hilt.

---

16   Quoted in *Le Passepoil*, 1947, p.6 – transcript of the arrêté du 13 germinal an II.

Plate 10
Pontonniers de Strasbourg ou Matelots Révolutionnaires 1793–1794 d'après la collection Boersch.[17]

Strasburg was, from the start a town with a fierce revolutionary zeal. There were many reasons to this. It had been French for barely over a century (since 1681), and it had a multi-cultural, or rather multi-religious, population of Catholics, Protestants, and Jews. It saw the liberal political and social changes as supporting its own diverse society and feared a possible backlash if a reactionary, arch-catholic monarchy came back to power.

Strasburg was also of course the main starting point for any French military force which had either to defend France from an attack from across the Rhine, or if it had to bring the conflict into German lands. Such military operations implied a technical challenge which the French army had rarely had to deal with in the past: having large units cross rivers, with the very first such obstacle being the Rhine.

There was in Strasburg a trade association of boatmen which early on offered their services to the Revolutionary government. In 1792, these men formed a battalion of pontonniers (bridge layers) composed of three companies. All their officers were elected, as was usually the case in that period for volunteers. When the French reached Mainz, the boatmen of that town also formed a battalion of pontonniers. Following the surrender of that town, that battalion and the Strasburg one were combined on 1 May 1794. It then took the name of Pontonniers et marins français révolutionnaires.

On 7 May 1795, as the overall artillery corps was being reorganised, the text clearly indicated that included eight companies of pontonniers; these were actually the eight existing pontonnier companies in Strasburg. From then on, the pontonnier battalion was located in Strasburg and dispatched companies to the various armies when required, in a similar fashion as to what was otherwise happening for the rest of the artillery. Much later, the battalion became a regiment in 1840 and left Strasburg only after the French defeat of 1871.

Its dress was logically patterned on that of the artillery but with some major specificities for the Revolutionary period.

Pontonniers de Strasbourg ou Matelots Révolutionnaires 1793–1794
Boisselier indicates as his source the Boersch paper soldiers. There are actually several contemporary sources, multiple paper soldiers series, and even some surviving headgear.

The pontonniers de Strasbourg were a well-known and popular unit in Strasburg, so they were well documented from the start. The Boersch series is probably quite accurate as Boersch not only used Zix's documentation but also knew veterans who could give him direct information on what they wore.

The overall uniform was that of the artillery with a few distinctive features: the cuff lapels were red piped white, so were the cuffs. The breeches and gaiters were Hungarian style with a red Hungarian knot. The officer also wore hussar-style breeches with rich gold lace. Note also the red waistcoats which seem to have been typical of the unit. Such red straight cut waistcoats were quite popular in Alsace with civilians at that time.

The oddest part of the uniform was of course the hat described also as Henri IV-style or a Corsican hat. This hat had a fairly wide brim raised on one side. That part could be worn on the side (as here) or upfront (reminding one of the late renaissance hats, hence the Henri IV style name).

---

17 Strasburg bridge layers or revolutionary sailors 1793–1794, after the Boersch collection. Dated June 1943.

On that upturned part there was a brass anchor ornament, a cockade and here also some lettering (pontonniers). A scarlet plume was also attached – some sources also give a red over black plume.

Two such hats have survived in public collections one in the Belgian army museum in Brussels, and another one in the French army museum. Such hats were actually quite popular with the Rhineland population, and this would explain its adoption by the pontonniers.

Plate 11
Sapeur 1793
Grenadier-gendarme près la convention nationale 1793–1794
Collection A de Marbot et Journal Militaire.[18]

Military engineers had been an important part not only the French military but of society at large. Given Louis XIV's intensive fortification works using Vauban's genius and leadership, the King's engineers had deeply modified border towns but also undertaken important civilian works. Yet, this select body of highly skilled professionals was part of the corps of artillery until the mid-eighteenth century. Even after that, it swung back and forth between being independent and back into the corps of artillery. Furthermore, during most of that period and until 1793, only the officers formed a separate body with a distinctive uniform. The men – sappers and miners – were part of the corps of artillery.

On 23 October 1793, the companies of miners were taken from the artillery and given to the engineers. Then on 15 December, a decree was enacted to form 12 sapper battalions each composed of eight companies of 200 men each.

Section III of the same decree provided details of the uniform for these sappers. It was to be the same as for artillery gunners but with yellow fringed epaulettes. The sappers were to be equipped with picks, spades, axes and any other tool they would require. As for their armament, they were given a short sabre and a pistol. They also had a black leather belt with a pistol holster and a small cartridge box. They were to wear either a hat or a helmet.

Interestingly, with this decision the corps of engineers was unique in the French army in having rank and file wearing a uniform different from that worn by its officers. Indeed, ever since the engineers had been separated from the artillery in 1758, the officers had worn a blue coat with black velvet as its distinctive colour. By 1786, this meant that engineer officers wore the usual French style blue coat with collar, cuffs, lapels in black velvet, and red turnbacks.

Over time, sappers and miners would eventually adopt the same uniform as their officers – the black velvet distinction on collar, cuffs, and lapels.

In 1789, when the third estate and some members of the nobility and clergy gathered in Versailles despite orders from the King not to do so, they were protected by guards from the Garde de la prévôté de l'hôtel (hotel provost's guard). This specific unit had as its main function to ensure order and security in all royal buildings. In so doing, they were the first unit from the royal household to side with what was to become the revolution. They continued to provide guards to what had become the National Assembly under their original title until 10 May 1791 when they were disbanded but immediately re-created as a specific company belonging to the new gendarmerie

---

18   Sapper 1793. Grenadier-gendarme of the National Convention 1793–1794. A. de Marbot collection and the Military Journal. Dated August 1943.

nationale under the name of Garde de l'assemblée nationale. In 1792, as the assembly had become known as the Convention, they became the Gardes de la convention and were now known as grenadiers-gendarmes près la convention nationale. These gendarmes-grenadiers were given the uniform of the gendarmerie but with the elite grenadier bearskin. Whether under the monarchy or in the early days of the revolution, they had only performed ceremonial, guard and at worst police duties. Although lacking any combat experience, they were nevertheless sent to the Vendée to help in suppressing the Royalist rebellion there. Their inexperience, coupled with the incompetence of their commanding officers and the general in charge, led to a total rout and they were almost completely wiped out and their flag was taken.

On 31 December 1793, the convention published a decree calling the unit back to Paris 'given the distinguished manner in which the brave grenadiers of the National Convention had behaved as out of 180, barely a third remains fit for service'.[19] This was putting a positive spin on a total disaster! It was put back up to strength and kept in Paris in its traditional role of guard and police duty for the legislative bodies. It evolved, along with a mounted unit as the Garde du directoire which was to be one of the major components in the future consular, and later Imperial Guard.

Sapeur 1793
Boisselier indicated as his source for the sapper both Marbot and the *Journal Militaire*. Indeed, he has copied Marbot's plate which shows a sapper as per the December 1793 decree. Marbot has given him a musket which Boisselier has not, sticking strictly with the decree. The yellow epaulettes are indeed somewhat striking, just as the absence of black coloured cuffs, cuff lapels, collar, and lapels. Again, this was the official regulation uniform which was probably adopted as these men had belonged to the artillery and it was easier for them to use their old coats, just adopting the yellow epaulettes.

Grenadier-gendarme près la convention nationale 1793–1794
The grenadier-gendarme is also taken from a Marbot plate and the *Journal Militaire*. There are some plates by Hoffmann, at least representing an officer from this little-known unit. His uniform is close to that adopted by the gendarmerie, which was to stay pretty much unchanged well into the first quarter of the nineteenth century: blue coat, red lapels, collar, cuffs, cuff lapels, with buff waistcoat and breeches and the distinctive buff lined white cross belts. The one difference with the gendarmerie is the white piping on the collar, lapels, cuffs and cuff lapels. The grenadier status is indicated by the wearing of a bearskin and red epaulettes. The bearskin has no plate and Marbot also shows in addition to the scarlet plume, a red racket and cord on the left side. Later, when becoming the Gardes du directoire, the unit was to adopt a dress somewhat similar to that of the line infantry with a bearskin and plate. In effect, this was the uniform worn afterwards by the grenadiers of the consular guard, and then later by the Imperial Guard.

---

19 *Archives Parlementaires volume de 1787 à 1860* (Paris: Paul Dupont, 1913), tome 82, p.502.

Plate 12
Garde nationale uniforme décrété le 19 juillet 1790, grenadier et chasseur, d'après une estampe originale de la bibliothèque du Roi.[20]

Pre-1789 France had a vast variety of military institutions. Aside from the regular army there was the much despised militia which was both its reserve and a form of army conscription, there existed several other militarized groups.

Many towns had set up milice bourgeoise (townsfolk militia) or what can best be described as shooting clubs, and sometimes both. The later had existed since the late Middle Ages to provide defence for the town or supplementary troops for the King. Often called compagnies d'archers (archer's companies) or compagnies de l'arquebuse (matchlock companies), their names related to bygone weapons and practices.

These various troops had still been quite active under the Sun-King Louis XIV providing occasional reinforcements for his multiple military campaigns. During the eighteenth century, the milice bourgeoise provided a police force in some towns, while the compagnies had turned into social clubs indulging at best in marksmanship contests and more frequently into just social gathering; drinking and singing.

In Paris, the milice bourgeoise, although supposedly still in existence, was no longer truly active while the compagnie de l'arquebuse had no dealings with policing the city. Ever since Louis XIV, and especially under Louis XV, an investigative police force had developed, and for more forceful needs, the Gardes Françaises and other such royal household or army troops were garrisoned in the town or nor far from it so they could be called upon in case of need.

During late June and early July 1789, the liberal Parisians who had started taking control of the town through the establishment of a Paris Commune realized that the situation was starting to get quickly out of control. These early revolutionaries had pretty much opened up a Pandora's box and hardly knew, not so much how to close it, but simply manage the forces they had unleashed on to the streets.

By 13 July 1789, the situation was such that the various military groups still in existence were proposing their services, in addition to which, pro-revolution soldiers were also gathering. On that evening it was decided to form a militia. As we know, on the next day the Bastille was stormed, and the revolution had officially begun with no turning back.

On 15 July, the King, as on so many other issues tried to take back the initiative by appointing general officers in command of this new Garde bourgeoise Parisienne. On the same day, in the town hall in a dramatic gesture typical of the period, one of the Commune members had pointed his index finger to a bust of La Fayette which the state of Virginia had sent as a present to the city and which was in that meeting room asking that 'the illustrious defender of freedom in the new world' be offered command.[21] On 16 July the King approved, and a few days later (18 July) La

---

20 National Guard uniform as decreed on 19 July 1790, grenadier and chasseur, after an original print in the King's library. Dated July 1943.
21 *Procès-verbal des séances et délibérations de l'assemblée générale des Électeurs de Paris, réunis à l'Hôtel de Ville le 14 juillet 1789, rédigé depuis le 26 avril jusqu'au 21 mai 1789, par M. Bailly et depuis le 22 mai jusqu'au 30 juillet 1790, par M. Duvergier* (Paris: Imprimeur de l'assemblée nationale, 1790), tome 1, p.422. This contemporary publication is a detailed almost minute by minute account of the official debates in the Paris town hall during the first year of the French Revolution.

Fayette agreed, provided his command was confirmed by a vote of the of the representatives of the Commune a few days later.

The permanent committee of the Commune, its executive body, had decided on 16 July to organize a military committee to determine the organisation of the militia, its clothing, supply etc. It had also indicated that 'in case other communes in the kingdom would wish to follow the example of Paris and organize similar citizen troops entrusted with their defence' that the newly formed militia would take the specific name of Garde nationale de Paris.[22]

The Garde nationale de Paris was, in effect born and as a consequence other local urban national guards were formed over the next few weeks and months. Typically, these troops would incorporate the various existing military organisations. By mid-1790, the previous institutions had virtually ceased to exist. Their formal dissolution was confirmed in the various decrees enacted during 1791 related to the organisation of the Garde nationale.

Interestingly, the Garde nationale de Paris went through at least three different uniforms until it settled for the final one, which in effect was similar to that of the line infantry. On 25 July 1789, the military committee had decided to set up six offices or sub-committees, each in charge of a different topic. The fourth office was to address the issue of clothing and weapons for both the infantry and the cavalry of the Garde nationale.

A first complete proposal for the guard had been submitted the day before by a member of the Feuillants (a Paris district) military committee. Douglas, a former student of a military school proposed as a uniform 'a red coat lined with red coarse cloth, blue turnbacks and cuffs with buttons bearing the Paris coat of arms and the words "Garde Parisiennes", a white waistcoat and breeches, black hat, the crown lined with black velvet, with a blue, red and white cockade and finally black gaiters.' This seemingly odd red coat faced with blue was actually quite similar to the one worn by the Paris compagnie de l'arquebuse which was scarlet faced with sky blue, but with a scarlet waistcoat and breeches. In effect this remained a proposal as on the morning of the 27 July, the fourth office came up with what was to become the first Garde nationale de Paris uniform:

> It has been agreed that the colour of the coat would be blue, its upright collar to be scarlet.
> Lapels, cuffs and lining to be white with red piping.
> waistcoat and breeches to be white.
> Buttons to be gilt.
> Cavalry will wear the same uniform but buttons and shoulder braid to be white.
> As for the cockade, the national colour being white, it is proposed it will be large and white with blue and red lining to show the colours of the town.
> The sword will be of yellow gilt metal for infantry, silver for cavalry.
> The gorget to be gilt with the town coat of arms.
> All leather equipment to be white.
> A town flag will be borne by each battalion with a distinctive legend adopted by each district. Each company will have a fanion[23]

---

22 *Procès-verbal des séances et délibérations de l'assemblée générale*, tome 2, p.50.
23 *Procès-verbal de la formation et des opérations du comité militaire étabi à l'hôtel de ville de Paris*, pp.19–20. This contemporary publication details all discussions related to the forming of the Garde nationale de Paris, 16–31 July 1789. Available at <https://gallica.bnf.fr/ark:/12148/bpt6k6264180z>.

This uniform was indeed worn and is shown in various period portraits, and prints. The cockade was soon to evolve into a more balanced red, white and blue split, as, over time the national colour was no longer to be white but actually the three national colours.

Other town national guards in France followed suit and in turn adopted an organisation and a uniform. In many cases, they simply copied the Paris uniform but with buttons or grenadier bearskin bearing a different motto or coat of arms. However, in a number of cases, the uniform colours were quite distinct and there were red, green, sky blue, or white coats worn by some town national guards.

On 14 July 1790, a massive gathering of national guards was organised in Paris on the Champ de Mars, in front of the military school and where the Eiffel tower stands today. Known as the fête de la fédération, it celebrated the federation of all national guards, and indeed each town national guard had sent some delegates. Aside from it being a pompous and sometimes awkward ceremony, it showed the huge diversity in dress of the various national guards. This lack of uniformity was certainly no statement of national unity.

Subsequently on 19 July 1790, the National Assembly decided that all national guards would wear the same uniform which is the one shown on this plate. Given the expenses that had been undertaken by the various towns, it was decided they had until the next celebration on 14 July 1791 to adopt the new uniform.

However, on 20 July 1791, a new and final uniform was adopted:

> The uniform of the national guards is finally ruled as follows:
> Royal blue coat, white lining, red piping, cuffs and collar scarlet with white piping; white lapels with scarlet piping, open sleeve with three small buttons, pockets on the outside with three pointed ends and three buttons piped red, button as per decree of last 23rd December [i.e. button of gilded copper with the words 'La Nation, La Loi, Le Roi' within a 'civic crown', i.e. laurel wreath, in between the crown and the edge 'District de…' and the name of the district] vest and breeches to be white.[24]

In fact, this uniform was more or less to become the regular infantry uniform as of January 1792. The main differences being over time that of adding cuff lapels.

Garde nationale uniforme décrété le 19 juillet 1790, grenadier et chasseur
Boisselier for this plate has chosen to represent the regulation uniform adopted on 19 July 1790 for all French Garde nationale units. We do know this was worn by Paris national guards as we have evidence of this from portraits, paintings, and some contemporary prints. In this specific case, Boisselier indicates he used as a source a print which was part of the King's library.

Both wear the blue coat with scarlet lapels, cuffs and coat tails, white collar piped red, while lapels and cuffs are piped white. The cut of the coat follows the 1786 regulation, so it is fairly loose and with a medium height collar. The grenadier has his typical scarlet braided epaulettes and carries a short sabre. There was no formal regulation pattern but one can easily imagine it to be of the well-known various Revolutionary types. It typically had a fairly large basket gilded hilt decorated with revolutionary symbols: For example, a Phrygian cap or a masonic pyramid. The bearskin cap is of

---

24 *Loi qui règle définitivement l'uniforme des gardes nationales, donnée à Paris le 20 juillet 1791*, two-page text, author's collection.

the short style which had been given back to line infantry in 1788. Previously the cap plate had on one side the royal crest consisting of an oval with three lilies on the left and one the right the town coats of arms. In Paris, it was the 'Paris ship', a medieval boat over water with the motto fluctuat nec mergitur (it floats but does not sink). With the generalization of a common uniform, the cap plate should have become what Boisselier shows here, a simple grenade. A tricolour braid and tassel and red plume finish off the bearskin decoration.

The chasseur is a more of an uncommon figure although we do have several portraits and period prints showing such an outfit. While the coat is the same as for the grenadier; the epaulettes are green with a red top braided circle. Green which is the chasseur colour (the regular army chasseur battalions wore green uniforms) is also visible at the tip of the plume, as the colour of the tassels which decorate the left and right hat corners. Finally green lace decorates the broad sash worn by the chasseur which doubles up as a holster for his pair of small pistols. The elite light status of this man is also displayed by his tight-fitting hussar-style blue breeches complete with red Hungarian knots and side piping along the legs. Finally, his gaiters simulate short Hungarian style boots. Such short gaiters were soon to become common place throughout the period for light infantry. Overall, this man's aspect is quite distinctive and certainly stands out. One must however be reminded that in effect this uniform was probably never really worn in actual combat, and only for policing activities within his home town.

Plate 13
Officier de la garde nationale
Soldat au 1er bataillon de la garde nationale de Paris
d'après le recueil de Léo (1794).[25]

> It is not easy to give any exact description of the national guards, nor can we classify them in any way. But one has to be convinced that they fight well; although one can find amongst them men wearing only coatees and shirts, blouses of rough cloth or coats of all shades of colour, civilian waistcoats with simple or Indian style embroidery, and breeches of all sorts. Most of them wear dark blue coats with red or white collars, buttons yellow or white stamped with a liberty bonnet or liberty tree. Some wear gaiters or cloth straps, many have shoes and silk stockings; but all have their hats decorated with small objects which evoke liberty and equality. They all have a musket and bayonet, some have cartridge boxes, others none. The same goes for a sword. Instead of a knapsack, they have a bag or cloth pocket in which they put they garments.[26]

The above is the description given in the text which was published along with the series of three plates in Leipzig in 1794 by Friedrich August Leo and which Boisselier has made an extensive use of. We have already seen the copies he made of former royal army grenadiers, here we have a national guard officer and a guard from the first battalion of the Garde nationale de Paris.

---

25 Officer in the National Guard. Soldier in the 1st Battalion of the Paris National Guard. Based on the Léo collection (1794). Dated June 1943.
26 *Description de quelques corps composant les armées françoises par un témoin oculaire – Abbildung und Befchreibung verfchiedener Truppen der franzöfifchen Armee mit illuminirten Kupfern* (Leipzig: Friedrich Auguft Leo, 1794), pp.8–9.

The first battalion was raised in the initial call to volunteers in 1791. At that stage, war had not yet been declared and there was still genuine zeal to support the Revolutionary but still royal government. The battalion fought in Belgium through 1792 and late into 1793. It then moved to Kleber's army in Mainz and this is probably where and when this officer and chasseur were seen.

The officers were, as usual, an interesting mix of young and even very young men in their twenties and mature if not senior individuals in their forties and even fifties! As this one man looks fairly young, one could imagine it was Jean-Charles Roussel, aged 20 from Paris. Roussel had been a gunner *caporal* in July 1791. By September 1793 he was a *lieutenant*. From 1793 to 1799 he was an aide to staff officers (adjudants-généraux). In 1799 he was a *chef de bataillion* in the 106e demi-brigade and its commander in 1800. He was a *général de brigade* in 1809 and was killed at Ostrowno in Russia on 26 July 1812. He had therefore risen from being a rank-and-file volunteer with no previous military experience to a general under the Empire.

As for the man, one could well imagine him to be Jean-François Moreau nicknamed 'monte-au-ciel' (rise to heaven) also aged 20, also from Paris. His nom de guerre probably derived from his recklessness in combat. He was a *sergent* by late 1793 but had a slower career than Roussel and was a *capitaine* by 1808 receiving the legion of honour. Moreau was wounded at Wagram and then Borodino, and eventually died in Vilnius in December 1812 after having been badly treated by Cossacks while being a prisoner and having managed to escape.

Interestingly enough, both men, although wearing the blue coloured coat of the Garde nationale de Paris, do have some odd features to their uniforms.

The officer has yellow cuffs while the chasseur has yellow lapels. Although some provincial national guards did have such colour combinations, this was not true for Paris. The original uniform was a blue coat with red collar, white lapels and turnbacks, white cuffs with red piping to the cuffs, lapels and turnbacks and finally yellow metal buttons.

Obviously by late 1793, many changes had occurred. The various inspections for the Garde nationale de Paris battalions often indicate the poor state of the clothing, and, as indicated in the text published with the plates, men would wear all kinds of outfits. It is probable that both this officer and the chasseur procured whatever coat they could get or had their original uniform mended as best as they could.

The officer also has a yellow waistcoat and a large black belt in which he has tucked a pistol. Indeed, officers were poorly armed, and they would often carry handguns. His tricolour breeches are typical of the Revolutionary fashion which can be observed in multiple contemporary prints and watercolours.

As for the chasseur, he does have green epaulettes denoting such status, but he has received a 1791 model helmet.

By 1794, the first battalion Garde nationale de Paris was to form the bulk of the 201e demi-brigade and thus became a line infantry unit and later becoming the 106e demi-brigade.

Plate 14
Carabinier du 6e bataillon de chasseurs à pied 1792
Chasseur 13e bataillon de chasseurs à pied 1791 (ex. Gardes Françaises)
d'après Victor et dessin contemporain.[27]

Light infantry was born in the eighteenth century out of the evolution of tactics in the various conflicts of the first half of that century. Apart from the large pitched battles and sieges, warfare also became one of raids and ambushes. The grenz (border) troops from Austria which excelled in this warfare, were soon copied by all European armies. During the Seven Years War (1756–1763), the French monarchy resorted to raising several units with the sole objective of undertaking what was called la petite guerre (the little war). Typically, they combined mounted and foot troops in one unit under the name legion. They wore distinctive dress, often inspired by exotic fashions: for example, Hungarian hussar-style or Pyrenees mountain dress.

The end of the conflict brought a reduction of the army, but some of these innovative formations were kept and survived in new volunteer or legion units. In 1776, these were formally integrated into the line army, mainly as chasseurs à cheval and chasseurs à pied. The cavalry units, set at 24 squadrons, were joined to dragoon regiments while the chasseurs à pied, as individual companies, were split across the 16 divisions in which the army was then organised.

In 1784, the mounted and foot chasseurs were again combined as six battalions of foot and six regiments of horse. Each combination formed a chasseur corps, bearing the name of a mountainous region of France: Alpes, Pyrénées, Vosges, Cévennes, Gévaudan, or Ardennes. This setup lasted only until 1788, when the six foot battalions were again separated and increased to 12. This was how they were organised when the revolution started, but essentially the future light infantry was born.

The chasseurs were from the start given a distinctive uniform which followed that of the infantry but which in colour reflected their origin and use: dark green for the coat, waistcoat and breeches. The 1786 regulation provided for distinctive colours for each battalion, but this was abandoned in 1788, when all adopted the daffodil colour. Also in 1788, buff-coloured breeches and waistcoats were distributed but do not seem to have had widespread usage, except for the waistcoats. There were other more subtle differences. The hat, quite similar to that of the line infantry was worn fore and haft and never transversely. In effect this provided a form of visor to the man. Men wore their hair long in a queue and never folded upwards in the 'catogan' fashion of the line infantry. Gaiters were shorter and rose up only to mid ankle. Finally, their muskets were shorter than those of the regular line infantry.

The 1791 regulation brought a number of changes which coincided with those of the line infantry. The 12 chasseurs battalions no longer used a name but were numbered from 1 to 12. Each was now to have a distinctive colour which would be shown at the collar, cuffs and cuff lapels. Green breeches were confirmed, but waistcoats now were white. As for the line infantry the Tarleton-style helmet was adopted.

In 1791, two new battalions were organised. These were raised from parts of the former Gardes Françaises which had been disbanded.

---

27 Carabinier of the 6th battalion of foot chasseurs 1792. Chasseur 13th battalion of foot chasseurs 1791 (formerly French Guards). After Victor and contemporary drawing. Dated June 1943.

As part of its evolving organisation, in 1788, the chasseurs battalions had created a new type of light infantryman, the carabinier. These were to be selected amongst the best men and more specifically the top marksmen in the battalion. Six of them were to be lined up with each company. As the name implied, they should have been armed with a carabine, which is the French word for a rifled musket. In the 1 April 1791 provisional dress regulation, the carabiniers were equated with the line infantry grenadiers receiving scarlet epaulettes and a bearskin cap, although slightly shorter and with no metal plaque. However, at about the same time, a revision of the light infantry organisation abolished them.

However, within a few months, with the advent of war, the chasseur battalions which were to become legions again were asked, as part of that decision, to set up a carabinier company for each battalion selecting their best men and arming them with rifled muskets. As it turned out the battalions were never really transformed into legions but participated in the formation of the new demi-brigades d'infanterie légère.

Carabinier du 6e bataillon de chasseurs à pied 1792
Chasseur 13e bataillon de chasseurs à pied 1791 (ex. Gardes Françaises)
Both these representations are based on drawings by Victor, a contemporary soldier. They were part of the large Dubois de l'Estang collection and were also copied by Raffet's son and used also by Marbot and Noirmont.

As indicated, carabiniers were only formally acknowledged in 1792. This man is armed, as per the 1792 decisions with a rifled musket. It sports a huge bayonet to compensate for its short length and the man is burdened with all the paraphernalia required to effectively load and use this marksman's weapon: ramrod, power horn, mallet. The Versailles arms factory only started producing rifled muskets in 1793, and so this one probably comes from a private manufacturer.

As per the 1791 regulation he has a short bearskin cap with visor, white cords and tassels and a red plume. Also, as per regulation, he has scarlet epaulettes. The sixth battalion had daffodil as a distinctive colour in 1791. This was to be worn as piping at the collar and cuff lapels. Here the collar is scarlet which is not in line with regulation but refers to the elite nature of the carabiniers and was to become the norm for both grenadiers and carabiniers. Also worthy of note are the daffodil straps for the epaulettes and the Hungarian-style gaiters with white lace and tassel.

The 13e bataillon chasseur is a former Garde Française. The two new battalions were given white as a distinctive colour. The 13e was to wear it on collar, cuffs and cuff lapels. As can be seen here, the cuff lapels are green. The distinctive colour was also worn at the bottom of the plume for the helmet which was worn only for parade dress. As per the 1791 regulation he has a white waistcoat and a helmet. The helmet style is however somewhat different from the norm, having a broad circular brim all around. There were actually many variations to the 1791 helmet given the multiplicity of manufacturers and this is probably one of them. One fairly odd feature is the wearing of white epaulettes. One can only assume that given that its origin was an elite unit (the Gardes Françaises), the battalion decided on adopting an elite characteristic such as epaulettes in their distinctive colour.

PLATE 1

Captain from the 75th Infantry Regiment, formerly Monsieur's, 1791–92. Marbot collection. Grenadier Drummer from the 102nd Infantry Regiment, after Victor.

See text for detailed plate commentaries.

PLATE 2

Troops of the line 1792–1793. Grenadier from the 1st Regiment of Line Infantry, based on a contemporary document from Breda. Fusilier from the 104th Regiment of Line Infantry, based on a contemporary drawing by Victor.

PLATE 3

Grenadier from the 67th Regiment of Line Infantry (formerly Languedoc) 1794 – Léo Collection. Sapper from the 82nd Regiment of Line Infantry (formerly Saintonge) 1791 – Original drawing by Victor, Dubois de l'Estang collection.

PLATE 4

Grenadier drummer of a line infantry demi-brigade 1795–1800, after an original drawing by Raffet. Grenadier of a line demi-brigade 1795–1800, after a mannequin in the Musée de l'Armée.

PLATE 5

Fusilier of a battle demi-brigade circa 1796. Officer of a battle demi-brigade circa 1796. Based on a German print from the Hennin collection, National Library, print room.

PLATE 6

Musician with the 32nd battle demi-brigade circa 1796. Boersch collection. Musician with the 57th battle demi-brigade 1798. Correspondence from General Victor Perrin to the Administration Board.

PLATE 7

Chasseur of the 14th light demi-brigade, year 6, Army of the Grisons. Drum-Major 18th line demi-brigade, year 6, Army of the Grisons. From contemporary watercolours by citizen François Muller. Hennin Collection, print room, National Library.

PLATE 8

Light infantry. Carabinier circa 1794 after Victor, Dubois de l'Estang collection. Chasseur circa 1793, after A. de Marbot and drawings by Raffet, French National Library.

PLATE 9

Balloonist and foot gunner, 1793. After the Dubois de l'Estang collection, drawing by Victor, Boersch collection etc. Lienhart and Humbert collection.

PLATE 10

Strasburg bridge layers or revolutionary sailors 1793–1794, after the Boersch collection.

PLATE 11

Sapper 1793. Grenadier-gendarme of the National Convention 1793–1794. A. de Marbot collection and the Military Journal.

PLATE 12

National Guard uniform as decreed on 19 July 1790, grenadier and chasseur, after an original print in the King's library.

PLATE 13

Officer in the National Guard. Soldier in the 1st Battalion of the Paris National Guard. Based on the Léo collection (1794).

PLATE 14

Carabinier of the 6th battalion of foot chasseurs 1792. Chasseur 13th battalion of foot chasseurs 1791 (formerly French Guards). After Victor and contemporary drawing.

PLATE 15

National volunteers battalions 1791–1792.
Contemporary drawings, Hennin collection, Carl collection, Würtz.

PLATE 16

Volunteers of the demi-brigades belonging to line troops in the army of Holland 1794–1795. From the Mellinet collection, print room of the National Library.

PLATE 17

Volunteers – Army of Holland 1795 – grenadier and fusilier sergeant. From the Mellinet collection, print room of the National Library.

PLATE 18

Grenadier volunteer and volunteer in the army of Holland 1794–1795. From the Mellinet collection, print room of the National Library.

PLATE 19

National Volunteers 5th Battalion of the Rhône 1793. Drum-major & grenadier, drawings from life by Victor.

PLATE 20

Volunteer Chasseurs of the city of Lyon 1794. Chasseur and drummer. Dubois de l'Estang collection.

PLATE 21

Volunteers of Santerre 1793–1794. Paris Volunteers 1793–1794. After Victor, Dubois de l'Estang collection, Army Museum.

PLATE 22

Marine Artillery, year 6 – Valmont collection. Black Legion, after Victor, Dubois de l'Estang collection.

PLATE 23

Foot Guide, Army of the Alps 1795–1796 – Document provided by Bernardin. Irish Legion 1796–1799 – A. de Valmont and Marbot.

PLATE 24

Byron Chasseurs 1792–1793. Southern Legion 1792–1794. After Victor, Dubois de l'Estang collection, Army Museum.

PLATE 25

1st Legion of the Franks 1796, grenadier and drummer. From the memoirs of General Bigarré, Striedbeck and the Boersch collection.

PLATE 26

Dutch Legion 1793 or Dutch Tirailleurs-Chasseurs according to documents of the period, Bréda Archives. Germanic Legion, foot chasseur 1792–1793 according to the work by Chuquet and Lienhart and Humbert collection.

PLATE 27

Piker of the Germanic Legion 1792–1794. Lienhart and Humbert and Chuquet's book on the Germanic Legion.

PLATE 28

Allobroges Legion created in 1792, drawing by Victor and A. de Marbot collection. Northern Legion 1793 – period document, Bréda archives.

PLATE 29

Grenadier, Legion of the Northern Francs 1799 – Lienhart and Humbert – Marbot, Military Journal. Grenadier, Danube Legion 1799 after a period print by Rugendas.

PLATE 30

Italic Legion, fusilier 8/9/1799, drawing by Martinet, Marbot, Lami, Military Journal.
Swiss demi-brigade 19/12/1798, Military Journal and contemporary coloured drawing.

PLATE 31

Grenadier of the auxiliary battalions 1799 created on 14 Messidor year 7 (2/7/1799)
Chasseur of the Northern Legion, 22 Fructidor year 7, Military Journal.

PLATE 32

Polish Legion circa 1798, after Hoffmann. Dombrowsky Legion after Victor.

PLATE 33

Paris Chasseurs 1794–1796. Westermann Legion 1792–1794 after Victor, Dubois de l'Estang collection, Army Museum.

PLATE 34

Paris Legion 1793–1794, after Victor, Dubois de l'Estang collection, Army Museum. Free Light Companies 1792, after Valmont, National Library.

PLATE 35

Basque Free Light Companies 1793, Basque Chasseur battalions (citizen Labouche's Basque Chasseurs, drawing by Lacauchie and watercolour from the National Library, prints).

PLATE 36

Free Legions of the West – carabinier and mounted chasseur, decree of the 3rd supplementary day of year 7 (19th September 1799) Military Journal.

PLATE 37

Trooper, 4th Regiment of Dragoons, circa 1794, Hennin collection. Trumpeter, 22nd Regiment of Dragoons, 1st Republic, Dubois de l'Estang collection.

PLATE 38

Commanding officer, line demi-brigade 1792–1794. After the Valmont collection.

PLATE 39

Carabinier drummer of the 1st light demi-brigade, circa 1798, Boersch collection. Heavy cavalry trumpeter, 1st Republic, Dubois de l'Estang collection.

PLATE 40

National Gendarmerie 1796 from an early print, print room. Carabinier 1794 from Leo's collection in Leipzig.

8th Cavalry Regiment or Cuirassiers Regiment 1792–1800. Formerly the King's Cuirassiers: Hoffmann, W.Kobell, Dubois de l'Estang collection.

PLATE 42

Trooper from the 2nd Cavalry Regiment 1793, based on a contemporary drawing executed in Breda. Trooper from the 19th Cavalry Regiment 1795, based on contemporary documents from Holland and Germany.

PLATE 43

Heavy cavalry trumpeter 1794 from a manuscript of the Mellinet collection, print room, National Library. Horse artillery gunner, 1792–1795 Military Journal and the A. de Marbot collection.

PLATE 44

Officer of the mounted chasseurs circa 1794 from the contemporary Leo collection. Trooper from the 5th Regiment of Mounted Chasseurs 1792, from the corps' recruitment poster of the unit.

PLATE 45

Mounted chasseur circa 1798 after a print by Steinlen. Mounted chasseur of the 9th Regiment 1795-1798 after a print in the National Library.

PLATE 46

Liberty Hussars 1792 – Captain. After Hoffmann and Marbot's collection.

PLATE 47

Liberty Hussars, 1st corps, trooper 1792 after Hoffmann. Mounted Chasseur Free Foreign Legion 1793 after a contemporary document from Breda.

PLATE 48

Non-commissioned officer in the Jemmapes volunteer hussars regiment, or Death Hussars, 1792–1793 – Boersch, Marbot, Lami and Martinet collection – later 10th Hussars.

PLATE 49

Mountain Hussars 1793 6 November. Alpine Hussars 1792. After the Lienhart and Humbert collection.

PLATE 50

Equality Hussars 1792 or Boyer Hussars in 1793, 6th Regiment. Fabrefonds' Hussars or Fabrefonds' Scouts 1792, in 1793, 8th Regiment. Lienhart and Humbert.

PLATE 51

Trooper from the 3rd Hussar Regiment 1794–1795 from the Mellinet collection, National Library, print room.
Trooper from the 4th Hussar Regiment 1794-1795 from the Mellinet collection, National Library, print room.

PLATE 52

2nd Liberty Hussars – trooper wearing a pelisse, war archives and Titeux 1793. Requisition Battalions 8 September 1793, Military Journal and print from the Hennin collection, print room of the National Library.

PLATE 53

Trumpeter of the 9th Hussars circa 1798 after Rugendas, National Library. Officer of the 7th bis Hussars circa 1796 after a contemporary print.

PLATE 54

1st Physician 1798 from Valmont's collection – National Library. Medical service driver, Lienhart and Humbert collection.

PLATE 55

Pharmacist 1798, after the Valmont collection, National Library. Surgeon Major 1798, after the Valmont collection, National Library.

PLATE 56

Naval gunner 17th class 1796-1802, Valmont. Company of 'men of colour' 1798-1800 Valmont.

Plate 15
Bataillons de volontaires nationaux 1791–1792
Dessins contemporains, collection Hennin, collection Carl, Würtz.[28]

After nearly two years of Revolutionary government, political tensions were rising both inside and outside of France. The King felt his power to be reduced beyond what could be tolerated. The anti-revolutionary party led from the neighbouring German lands by the King's brothers continued to get support both from the pro-monarchy French who were emigrating but also from other monarchs. That mighty France had been weakened by an unstable political situation was one thing, but that it would descend into chaos with possible far-reaching consequences was another.

In early 1791, the National Assembly started to bring the army back to war-ready strength and, having abandoned the old militia system which provided ready reserves, called for a recruitment of 100,000 auxiliaries. By June 1791, it was obvious that neither endeavour had had any success. On the 13 June, the assembly called for volunteer conscription from the Gardes nationaux to a level of one volunteer for 20 guards.

Eight days later, the King tried to escape from France to join his brothers and recapture his lost power. The immediate consequence was that the Garde nationale was fully activated on 21 June. On 13 July, another decree stipulated that the Garde nationale was to supply 26,000 men for new mobilized battalions. These decisions were at the origin of the first volunteer levy.

On 4 August 1791, the total amount of required Garde nationale volunteers was set at 107,000, which amounted to 187 new battalions. The situation was to evolve again the following year after the declaration of war. Having to face the combined forces of Austria and Prussia, on 11 July 1792, the assembly declared that the fatherland was in danger and called on all volunteers to assemble in Paris.

These volunteers of 1791 and 1792 formed units independent from the regular army. Whereas there was genuine enthusiasm in 1791, there was much less in 1792, at least until July.

Volunteer battalions had a poor reputation as most of the men were raw recruits with very little, if any, training. Officers were appointed through elections as volunteer units' regulations called them to appoint their own officers. Furthermore, the very same volunteer unit regulations indicated that they could leave their units with a two months-notice period. Such notice period existed to ensure they could be replaced, which of course did not really happen. All this resulted in volunteer units having poor discipline.

As stated by countless testimonials, the officers often had rarely been chosen by their men for their military proficiency but more for their aptitude at giving a good rousing speech, offering ample supplies of beverages and, at best, adequate revolutionary fervour. Their lack of discipline made them quite unwanted in many towns and as *lieutenant-général* de la Morlière who commanded the 21e division wrote about the volunteer battalion from Allier which had assembled in the town of Moulins: '

> I have the honour to advise you of the lack of discipline which resides in this unit and beg you to point out to me a form of punishment efficient enough to have these volunteers adopt obedience and respect for authority which is required from any soldier … However

---

28 National volunteers battalions 1791–1792. Contemporary drawings, Hennin collection, Carl collection, Würtz. Dated May 1943.

you consider it, the town citizens wish that this troop leaves as their misconduct is of worry to them.[29]

The newly formed départements which had replaced the old provinces were to supply them with adequate clothing, weapons, and other equipment. This they often failed to do.

Despite all this, the volunteers did survive the first year of war and in their ranks one found men who would distinguish themselves and achieve the highest ranks in the years to follow, such as the future Napoleonic *maréchal* Gouvion Saint-Cyr or Berthier's future aide-de-camp and famous painter, Lejeune.

Bataillons de volontaires nationaux 1791–1792
No specific uniform was determined for the volunteer battalions, other than that which had been decided for the Garde nationale by July 1791. In effect, the volunteers, when they received clothing, wore typical Garde nationale uniforms. It could be the blue faced red uniform of 1790, the original Paris-style uniform of 1789, or even the recently decided blue faced white with red collars and cuffs of 1791.

Boisselier quotes contemporary drawings in the Hennin collection in the Bibliothèque nationale de France and the Wurtz paper soldier collection as sources for his plate. The man on the left is probably a former chasseur from a Garde nationale unit given his green epaulettes. He wears a coat which is in line with the 1791 regulation except for its white cuff lapels, and white metal buttons. In much later years, the Garde nationale would distinguish itself by wearing white metal buttons and lace, but in 1791–1792, buttons were of yellow metal. However, some Garde nationale units had chosen white metal in 1789 for their buttons.

The drummer is also a chasseur drummer given his epaulettes and short tufted plume on the hat. The lace shown on the drummer's coat sleeves is interesting in that it shows a tricolour arrangement somewhat similar to that which existed in line infantry regiments with the King's livery. Boisselier indicates that he copied this from a Hoffmann plate which is an excellent and very reliable period source.

Plates 16, 17, & 18
Volontaires des ½ brigades des troupes de ligne à l'armée de Hollande 1794–1795
Volontaires – Armée de Hollande 1795 – grenadier et sergent de fusiliers
Grenadier volontaire et volontaire à l'armée de Hollande 1794–1795
d'après la collection Mellinet, cabinet des estampes de la bibliothèque nationale.[30]

The following three plates have to be presented together as they are drawn from the same source, which was also used for a few cavalry types. This source, sometimes known as the album de Mellinet, is a set of 70 superb watercolours of obvious contemporary manufacture preserved in the Bibliothèque nationale de France. To these, one must add sets of very fine prints which duplicate in

---

29 Quoted in Camille Rousset, *Les volontaires 1791-1794* (Paris: Didier, 1870), pp.18–19.
30 Volunteers of the demi-brigades belonging to line troops in the army of Holland 1794–1795. Volunteers – Army of Holland 1795 – grenadier and fusilier sergeant. Grenadier volunteer and volunteer in the army of Holland 1794–1795. From the Mellinet collection, print room of the National Library. Dated November, June, and November 1943

part the watercolours but add a few more figures. The complete series is probably a run of 20 plates but there is no hard proof of that.

In total, they are the most comprehensive iconographic depiction of a French Revolutionary army on campaign. How they seem to have come to be and how they were handed down to us is in itself a story worthy of the Revolutionary and post-Revolutionary times.

At the very end of 1794, *général de division* Charles Pichegru pushed his army into Holland and by late January 1795, he had conquered the old United Provinces with a crowning improbable (and possibly apocryphal) victory: the capture of the Dutch fleet by a squadron of the 8e hussars and a battalion of light infantry (the Belgian tirailleurs), as the boats stood immobilized by frozen water and the cavalry could just ride up to them!

Whereas in the seventeenth and early eighteenth century, Holland had been a haven of peace for French intellectuals who had often taken refuge in the Dutch Republic and printed works otherwise censored in France, the situation had to a large degree reversed itself. The Republic was now one in name only, and power was concentrated more and more in the hands of the Stadhouder, a position which was held firmly by the family of Orange-Nassau. In practice, the United Provinces were more a monarchy than a republic.

A first attempt at a revolution was made in 1785 but was put down with the help of Prussia. Although officially neutral, the alignment of Holland with Prussia and Austria could only lead to war with France. Dutch patriots were prominent in Paris and supported acts against the Dutch government. It was with no surprise that war was declared by France in 1793.

Pichegru was probably one of the most brilliant generals to have emerged from the revolution. He came from very low origins; his parents were peasants in the Jura mountains in the east of France, just above Switzerland. He had proven to be intellectually gifted and had studied in the military school in Brienne. There he had come across the young Bonaparte who was eight years younger. Pichegru had been his repetiteur (tutor) in mathematics. A *sergent* in the artillery, Pichegru quickly rose with the revolution. His exceptional analytical skills and quick decision-making abilities worked wonders. The conquest of Holland was to be one of his most memorable feats.

As Pichegru's army marched into Holland, it was still made up of the old (by now) volunteer troops of 1793–1794 and it presented a fairly surprising aspect to the locals, who were more used to the strict disciplined looks of the Prussian and Dutch armies. Furthermore, the French were not as a whole perceived as invaders, but to a large degree as liberators, as a sizeable portion of the Dutch were in favour of the patriots. Quickly the Batavian Republic was established and for the next 17 years, Holland was to be closely aligned with France, up to the point of being incorporated into the French Empire in 1810.

In Rotterdam in 1794, lived a German artist from Mannheim, August-Christian Hauck, 51 years of age. He had been living in Holland for a few decades by then and had become an official citizen of the town in 1776. He was a portrait painter and had taken on students who also acted as his aides. One of them, Cornelis Bakker had married one of his daughters. Together they also produced prints. It is thanks to their combined initials which can be found on the series of prints that we can attribute these watercolours to Hauck and possibly Bakker. As they observed Pichegru's men in the winter of 1794–1795, they took note of them and chose to produce from these a series of prints which were hand coloured and put on the market.

The series of prints seems to have been of 20 plates. A complete set is in the Anne S.K. Brown Collection in the United States. It can easily be checked online. Another, less extensive set of 16 plates was in the Brunon collection and is now in another private French collection.

Sepia coloured wash drawings seem to have also been the property of Gabriel Cottreau, a famous collector, at the turn of the twentieth century, but we have no knowledge of their current whereabouts. Some of the plate types were not part of the watercolours series which leads us to believe that some of the original paintings have long since gone missing.

As for the watercolours, they were first heard of when they were in the collection of *général de division* Émile Mellinet. Born in 1798, he had started as a 16-year-old junior officer in the 1814 campaign and then went on to a very distinguished career which led him to commanding the Imperial Guard infantry in Crimea and Italy under the Second Empire. He also had some artistic traits, being known as a music composer, and a large collector of books, and autographs. Although he had left his military library to the ministry of war, this did not include his iconographic collection which went up for sale. How he had come across this album of watercolours is unknown. It was purchased by another bibliophile, Auguste Lesouef. His sister had married an Englishman, Jules Smith and his nieces ended up being close to him and so inherited his estate. In 1913 they gave the entire print collection to the French state and that is how the album ended up in the Bibliothèque nationale de France.

Ever since then, along with the prints, it has been copied by all modern artists. In the Brown Collection, one can find a series of Boisselier watercolours which is an extensive copy of it. Leliepvre also did a full copy. So did Rousselot, the Funckens and others. All major artists with an interest in Revolutionary armies used it at some stage in their various works.

It is unique in that it really shines as a quasi-photographic image of the French Revolutionary soldiers on campaign given the very high artistic quality of both paintings and prints and their extreme precision. Some figures look fairly extravagant and yet Boisselier did not reproduce them in this series. However, other contemporary iconography confirm such oddities.

Volontaires des ½ brigades des troupes de ligne à l'armée de Hollande 1794–1795
The volunteer on the left wears a typical brown civilian coat. It is only in 1806 that French infantrymen were formally and universally issued with greatcoats. In a few prior cases, they had been provided with such items of dress, but this was done at the unit or army level. The early armies of the Republic had no such provision in place and so the men had to procure whatever they could to shield themselves from poor weather conditions. Holland in the winter was no warm place. One can assume that this man is a grenadier given the small scarlet epaulettes he has. He seems to be wearing only a waistcoat under his greatcoat and one can see his large civilian shirt collar emerging with a civilian ribbon-tie. Boisselier has shown some black inner leg patches either as a reinforcement or more probably some form of repair. None of the figures in the prints or watercolour series show this. It is possible that Boisselier took this from another source or simply made a mistake when copying the figure.

On the right is another grenadier volunteer with a typical set of civilian breeches. He wears a coat with shortened coat tails. This is probably more due to having them being damaged and so repaired by simply cutting them short. The fact that the coat has red and not white lapels indicates that this is probably one of the original Garde nationale coats issued back in 1790–1791, which also fits with it having being damaged with extensive use. The man carries a typical Revolutionary sabre with a basket hilt quite common in the 1790s.

Volontaires – Armée de Hollande 1795 – grenadier et sergent de fusiliers
With these two men, a grenadier and a *sergent* we go back to somewhat slightly more regulation looking individuals, although quite a few details indicate campaign adaptations.

The grenadier has a civilian waistcoat and breeches with short black gaiters. One of his cross belts are in natural tan leather and the other one in black. His hat is protected with a green oilskin cover. Such an item was fairly common throughout the period and is amply shown in the Hauck watercolours and prints.

The *sergent* on the right has adopted greenish cavalryman type breeches with black inner leg leather reinforcements. Like one of the previous types we have described he wears a coat with shortened coat tails which seem to be an old 1790–1791 Garde nationale model. The *sergent* also has the green oilskin cover for his hat and a black shoulder belt for his sabre.

Grenadier volontaire et volontaire à l'armée de Hollande 1794–1795
Boisselier conceived this plate probably to show the contrasts which existed in Pichegru's army. On the left we have a volunteer grenadier in a quasi-regulation full dress. His coat is exactly as it should be, following the 1791 coat design (down to the cuff lapels). He has a short grenadier bearskin, again very much as per the 1791 regulation. The only extravagance is the tricolour plume with ribbons. Only the black shoulder belt for the sabre does not fit the otherwise perfect look of this man.

By contrast the man on the right is one of the most famous types shown in the Hauck series. He seems to be wearing a type of carmagnole, a short jacket, possibly made out of an old regulation military coat. He also has a white waistcoat. For the rest, he has obviously procured items from the local Dutch. His baggy red trousers, white and blue gaiters are typical of the Dutch as are of course his wooden shoes. To protect him from the cold he has a woollen blanket and a pale blue knitted cap. From a distance, if it were not for his weapons, he could be taken for some Dutch peasant. Finally, his white cross belts have been replaced by natural leather ones, again probably procured locally.

Plate 19

Volontaires nationaux 5e bataillon du Rhône 1793
Tambour-Major & Grenadier, dessins d'après nature de Victor.[31]

In 1792–1793, volunteers were raised across France and there was genuine patriotic enthusiasm in some regions. The Rhône and Loire département which actually covered both the Lyon area and the mountainous region west of it where the Loire river takes its source provided five battalions of volunteers.

The 5e bataillon was part of the armée du Nord in 1793–1794 and that is when men from it were seen by the soldier Victor, who left watercolours which were copied by several artists including Raffet's son. Raffet's copies which are in the Bibliothèque nationale de France show three types of grenadiers and two of *tambour-majors*.

Although at first glance they do not seem to present any major difference with the typical French Revolutionary infantryman's dress, closer observation actually reveals a striking and unique difference.

---

31   National Volunteers 5th Battalion of the Rhône 1793. Drum-major & grenadier, drawings from life by Victor. Dated May 1943.

Their coat is blue with red cuffs and collar, white turnbacks and lapels. However, all these features have what is a yellow lace for the grenadiers and probably a gold one for the *tambour-majors*. Even more intriguing is the odd cut of the lapels. Instead of being the traditional wide and open cut above the waist, the lapels end straight above the waistline. The bottom of the lapels is also laced yellow or gold. This still leaves the white shirt visible. The coat cut looks like a precursor of the future habit-veste coat which was to become fashionable later and adopted with the 1812 regulation.

Volontaires nationaux 5e bataillon du Rhône 1793, tambour-major & grenadier
There are few period representations of *tambour-majors* for the early revolutionary period. This is one of the few we have and although he does stand out from the rank and file thanks to his richly laced uniform, it still is far less extravagant than what will be seen under the First Empire. The coat is similar to that worn by the grenadier except for its lace which is probably gold. Two laces indicate *sergent* rank on the forearms. He has large epaulettes which do not denote a rank but are more to have him stand out. They are gold but the threads are mixed blue and gold. His breeches are blue with a fancy Hungarian gold lace. Boisselier's rendering of it is actually fairly simple and Raffet's copy shows a more intricate design. He has red leather Hungarian boots with gold lace – again Raffet's copy also shows a small gold tassel for each boot. His hat is not laced but carries a large red plume with a base of white and blue plumes. His baton is given as silver or white metal by Boisselier but the Raffet copy shows yellow metal which is more logical given the gold lace and buttons.

As for the grenadier on the right, except for the odd cut of the coat lapels, he offers a very regulation profile. Boisselier has chosen not to show this too openly by having his grenadier with his arms hiding the bottom of the lapels.

Plate 20
Chasseurs volontaires de la ville de Lyon 1794
Chasseur et tambour
Collection Dubois de l'Estang.[32]

The excesses of the arch-centralized Jacobin revolutionary government fuelled not only the counter-revolutionary Royalist insurrection in the west, but also other rebellions in France. Moderates who had previously supported the revolution could not bear the dictatorial regime of the terror and joined forces with the royalists to oppose the radical republic.

Such was the case for the city of Lyon which rebelled and withstood a ferocious siege in the fall of 1793. It finally surrendered and was to be totally destroyed. Fouché, Napoleon's future police minister was in charge of the repression, and he had some 2,000 rebels shot. Lyon's name was not to be used, but ultimately, being a major city and an important economic centre, it survived this ordeal.

Unfortunately, little if anything is known of this volunteer unit. It is documented in one of the volumes of the Dubois de l'Estang collection currently in the Invalides reserves. Several bound leather volumes show pen or pencil black and white fine drawings of various units from the

---
32 Volunteer Chasseurs of the city of Lyon 1794. Chasseur and drummer. Dubois de l'Estang collection. Dated June 1943.

revolution to the Empire, along with a description of the colours. Their style implies they were done probably in the 1820s–1830s. In some cases, such as this one they show an otherwise totally unknown and undocumented unit. Its overall aspect is however quite plausible. This unit was probably raised after the siege of Lyon from local patriots to show their support of the Republican government.

Chasseurs volontaires de la ville de Lyon 1794, chasseur et tambour
The overall uniform style is that of the light infantry: pointed cuffs and lapels, breeches with Hungarian knot, and short Hungarian style gaiters. The main uniform colour used is dark blue and the distinctive colour is yellow which over time will also be distinctive for light troops (voltigeurs) just like green. Lapels are yellow and the shirt is also laced with yellow. Being chasseurs they have green and yellow epaulettes. The plume on the hat is yellow and red which may indicate that this man may be elite.

The drummer wears the same uniform as the chasseur, but with a green and yellow plume. As a drummer he has yellow swallow's nests and yellow laces on his coat sleeves. This was a common design for drummers in the old royal army and would still be seen under the First Empire.

Plate 21
Volontaires de Santerre 1793–1794
Volontaires de Paris 1793–1794
D'après Victor, collection Dubois de l'Estang, Musée de l'Armée.[33]

Again, little is known about the two units represented on this plate. However, they are shown both in the Dubois de l'Estang volumes, and in the Marbot and Noirmont plates, therefore confirming what they looked like.

Both the volontaires de Santerre and the volontaires de Paris were raised from the Parisian population in 1793 for service in the Vendée against the Royalist insurrection; 12,000 such volunteers marched out, organised in various units.

Antoine-Joseph Santerre was a Parisian brewer who had participated in the storming of the Bastille on 14 July 1789. From then on, his career was that of a true revolutionary firebrand. An officer in the Garde nationale de Paris, he became its commander in September 1792, but relinquished this position to become a general in the Vendée in June 1793, partly to escape from the excesses of the terror. By no means a professional soldier and with poorly trained troops his performance was far from adequate. He was called back to Paris and imprisoned in September 1793. The fall of Robespierre in the summer of 1794 released him from prison. He had lost all his fortune, and his wife had left him. Despite his efforts to again make some money from dealings with the army, he did not succeed and died still bankrupt in 1809.

The Santerre volunteers were named after him and were part of his force, along with other Parisian volunteer units. The text which accompanies the plate in Marbot and Noirmont's volume states the following:

33　Volunteers of Santerre 1793–1794. Paris Volunteers 1793–1794. After Victor, Dubois de l'Estang collection, Army Museum. Dated August 1943.

In May 1793, the Commune of Paris decided to raise from within the boundaries of the capital, an army of 12000 men to march on to the Vendée. It was within these battalions called the '500 livres heroes', thus named because of the amount of the enlistment bounty they received, that were the Paris volunteers and the Santerre volunteers. These units, a gathering of the most vile population brought to the army, not warlike dispositions, but a lack of discipline and a taste for looting. They were in great part the reason why the Republican army was defeated.[34]

As volunteers, they were to be dressed as light units and so adopted light infantry features such as pointed cuffs. As they were somewhat improvised, they used 1791 helmets from the stores and brown cloth which could readily be obtained.

Both units had a brown coat with yellow-buff collars. The Paris volunteers had buff as a distinctive colour for cuffs and lapels, while the Santerre volunteers had red. Both received white woollen epaulettes. Like the Garde nationale de Paris chasseurs, they had a large red cloth waistbelt in which they tucked two small pistols. They had buff-coloured breeches with Hungarian knots. They wore the ubiquitous but unpopular 1791 helmet. It is probable that the actual aspect of those volunteers was far from being as smart as that shown by Boisselier or Marbot.

Plate 22
Corps d'artillerie de Marine, An IV – Recueil de Valmont
Légion Noire, d'après Victor, collection Dubois de l'Estang.[35]

Naval troops and uniforms are one of the least documented topics in France. Luckily, during the first half of the nineteenth century, Valmont, a naval officer with a passion for uniforms undertook a massive study on French army and navy uniforms which he left to the Bibliothèque nationale de France. His watercolours have been a huge source of information for artists, especially for the navy as he was an eyewitness to his times (1820s–1870s) but also had access to information and documents which have since disappeared.

Naval artillery as an independent branch of service was created in 1792 and then formed into demi-brigades on 9 Brumaire year IV (9 October 1795). Boisselier's figure is a direct copy of the Valmont watercolour showing the naval artillery and infantry in 1795. There are two differences with the regular field artillery: the turned down collar, which is typical of the period in terms of fashion but not necessarily in some regular army uniforms, and the black leather equipment, which is typical of naval troops.

The légion noire was actually the légion des francs de Mayence – legion of the Mainz Franks – which was raised in April 1793 from volunteers who were besieged in the town of Mainz. The source for it is again, the Dubois de l'Estang volumes.

The légion des francs de Mayence figure on the right wears a grey uniform distinguished with black. He has a Corsican hat. As we saw earlier, such hats were quite popular in the Rhineland area. This sombre uniform is somewhat similar to that adopted much later by the real légion noire, which has resulted in the two units been sometimes confused.

---

34 E. de Noirmont and Alfred de Marbot, *Costumes Militaires Français* (Paris: Clément, 1860), tome 3, p.9.
35 Marine Artillery, year 6 – Valmont collection. Black Legion, after Victor, Dubois de l'Estang collection. Dated July 1943.

Plate 23
Guide à pied, armée des Alpes 1795–1796 – Document Bernardin
Légion Irlandaise 1796–1799 – A. de Valmont et Marbot.[36]

This plate shows two units which only have in common the fact they are almost totally unknown but can be considered as the ancestors of troops which achieved quite some fame under Napoleon.

Guide à pied, armée des Alpes 1795–1796
Boisselier found the source for this extremely colourful figure in a short article published in October 1925 in the *La Giberne* bulletin. It was one of the last studies done by Léonce Bernardin, today a completely forgotten figure, but at the time was then known to militaria enthusiast as an avid researcher who could dig deep into archives and libraries to come up with scarce and otherwise unknown information. Bucquoy described him as an 'old library rat', who actually really looked physically like one!

True to his usual self, he had found in the war archives information about this unit which was partially the origin of the armée d'Italie Guide à pied, later to become the Guides à pied de l'armée d'Orient, and even later the chasseurs à pied of the consular guard.

Guide units were an essential part of any staff organisation during the Revolutionary and Napoleonic wars. Maps were scarce and hard to come by, and even when they existed, they could often be obsolete or worse, totally wrong. Intelligent men familiar with the environment and if possible fluent in the local language were therefore much in demand. Given the mountainous nature of the terrain where it operated, the armée des Alpes needed foot and not mounted guides. Kellermann, who had been put in charge of the army in December 1792, had found at his service a troop of excellent horsemen but they proved quite useless as they also knew nothing of the area!

By April 1793, he had pulled together a band of some 30 foot guides: poachers, smugglers, and hunters who knew every inch of the land, were excellent marksmen and smart enough to take the initiative when needed. Over time the unit was to be expanded to 100 men, all were raised locally and commanded by a *capitaine*. At most it mustered some 80 men and for three years operated in the Tarentaise and Maurienne valleys. They were undertook police duty, acted as couriers, and guided troops. In June–July 1797 the unit was transferred to the armée d'Italie and from there moved on to the armée d'Orient.

Its uniform was set on 20 April 1795 and is described in detail. This is what was used by Boisselier for his reconstruction:

> Sky-blue hussar-style coat with red piping, turnbacks and cuffs
> Red undercoat
> Sky-blue Hungarian style breeches
> Black half-gaiters, grey half-gaiters
> Forage cap, sleeved coat, both sky-blue
> All buttons and lace white
> Armament: short 1783 musket (musketoon), infantry sabre
> Equipment: Corsican style cartridge box, infantry knapsack and mail bag.[37]

---

36 Foot Guide, Army of the Alps 1795–1796 – Document provideed by Bernardin. Irish Legion 1796–1799 – A. de Valmont and Marbot. Dated August 1943.
37 Léonce Bernardin and Pierre Bénigni, 'Guides à pied de l'armée des Alpes', *La Giberne*, October 1925, pp.27–28.

During the course of 1795, the guides received material to have some hussar caps made with plumes and braiding. Officers had the same outfit, but also had a braided dolman, but no pelisse. This was probably used only for full dress. Boisselier's gouache closely follows the written description and the black and white illustration by Benigni featured in *La Giberne*.

The coat was the typical light cavalry undress coat with pointed cuffs and lapels. The cartridge box was worn on the belly, Corsican style. One can spot the leather mail bag worn across the right shoulder. Boisselier has imagined that the hussar cap has a red flame just like the piping and cuffs. The plume is tricolour as befitting men attached to headquarters.

Légion Irlandaise 1796–1799
This figure is labelled as Légion Irlandaise which is quite ironic as it never bore that name and most of its men were not Irish! Boisselier's mistake is, however, quite understandable as he used Marbot's plate 52 in the third volume and Valmont's watercolours as his source. Both use the name Légion Irlandaise. Marbot which shows only an officer, in his text indicates as a creation date November 1790, which is an obvious mistake. Valmont gives the same date and copied the officer, adding an enlisted man.

There is further confusion due to the fact that, as of 1803, Napoleon raised an Légion Irlandaise which over time would become the 3e régiment étranger and achieve some fame.

Historically the French royal army had a long history of employing Irish troops. The Brigade Irlandaise as it was known had a splendid fighting record. When all the foreign regiments were transformed into French units, Dillon became the 87e, Berwick the 88e and Walsh the 92e. Many of the officers of Irish descent were quite loyal to the Bourbon family and sought refuge in emigration, even fighting against the Republic wearing British uniforms!

The French Republic had quite a loathing of foreign troops, but it came to realize, as the French monarchs had done before, that Ireland was a weak point for Britain. Between 1796 and 1798, it mounted two expeditions to try and invade Ireland, but these were dismal failures, even though the last one in 1798 achieved some measure of success.

In 1796, *général de division* Hoche proposed to mount an invasion and to that purpose proposed to raise a free foreign legion actually named the brigade étrangère. It was organised on 12 Brumaire Year 5 (3 November 1796) in Morlaix, Brittany. It was composed of four regiments made up from elements coming from various demi-brigades. Each regiment was to have two battalions, each composed of eight fusilier and one grenadier company. There were some foreign men, and even some Irish, but the vast majority were French and the idea was that once landed in Ireland, it would complete its ranks with Irish volunteers who would flock to the service of their liberators!

The regiments were known by the name of their respective commanders: Ferdut (1er and 3e grenadier companies from the 107e ligne), La Châtre (2e and 3e grenadier companies, 17e ligne), Lee (1e grenadier company 39e ligne, 3e grenadier company 107e ligne) and O'Meara (2e grenadier company, 9e ligne and 1e grenadier company 17e ligne). As one can guess from their names, Lee and O'Meara were of Irish stock, but both had been born in France. Just prior to embarking in 1798, the brigade had only 623 men: 102 for Lee's, 230 for Ferdut's, 133 for O'Meara's and 158 for La Chatre's. It was finally disbanded on 21 February 1799.

The only sources we have for the uniforms worn by the brigade étrangère are Marbot's plate and Valmont's watercolour. Boisselier used mainly Valmont as a source. The uniform is red faced green. Red was indeed the colour used by the Irish regiments of the royal army, but none had green as its distinctive colour. It was however an obvious choice being the traditional Irish colour. One will note that the coat has a turned down collar typical of the period, but not usually seen on enlisted men's clothing. This could actually be a mistake made by Valmont who might have just copied the officer's coat. The cuffs are simple and straight with no cuff lapels. Although all the men composing the original units came from grenadier companies, there are no red epaulettes, but the hat does bear the grenadiers' red plume.

Plate 24
Chasseurs de Byron 1792–1793
Légion du Midi 1792–1794
D'après Victor, collection Dubois de l'Estang, Musée de l'armée.[38]

Again, the sources for these two figures come from sketches by Victor which are in the Dubois de l'Estang collection and a copy of which was done by Raffet's son and are in the Bibliothèque nationale de France.

These are typical of the light units which were raised as needed on the French borders.

Chasseurs de Byron 1792–1793
This unit actually has existed under two names the Chasseurs du Rhin and the légion de Biron. The eastern border along the Rhine was obviously the most at risk when war broke out in the spring of 1792. Local commanding general officers were allowed to raise units by a decree dated 25 July 1792. It was determined the units were to use rifles which had been manufactured in Belgium in Liège in 1790 and were readily available. These were sent to the Rhine region and as a consequence it was determined the units were to be chasseurs. Their uniform was not specified but it was to be procured in the most economical manner and colour. We know from Victor's sketch as well as from a plate by Marbot that the uniform chosen made them look like Tyrolean Jäger and precursors of many of the British rifle units. It was entirely dark green with black leather equipment and a Corsican hat. They had a sword-bayonet and they also carried a short lance with a hook which they used to position their rifle and take aim more comfortably. They also attached a small wooden mallet to their black cartridge belt. It was used to force down the bullet into the grooved barrel.

This unit was not composed of raw volunteers but actually received men who had previously served in the recently disbanded Swiss regiments. *Lieutenant-général* Biron had organised them, hence the name. The various companies were grouped into two battalions under the command of *lieutenant-colonel* Pierre-Barthelemy Ferino. He was a seasoned veteran, and a native of Piedmont. Like his father, he had served in the Austrian army but ill-pleased with his career and attracted to the ideals of the revolution, he had come to France to offer his services. The unit fought in the Alsace area for all of its existence despite the fact that Biron, after having been promoted to the armée des Alpes, requested it. On 19 June 1795, the chasseurs du Rhin were incorporated into the 16e bis infanterie légère demi-brigade – therefore becoming regular light infantry.

Légion du Midi 1792–1794
The word midi actually means south in French. The Légion du Midi was officially organised under that name by a law dated 21 July 1792 and by a decree dated 8 September 1792. It had actually been

---

38   Byron Chasseurs 1792–1793. Southern Legion 1792–1794. After Victor, Dubois de l'Estang collection, Army Museum. Dated August 1943.

by *général de division* Montesquiou in early July 1792 in Antibes on the riviera and it was sent at the end of August 1792 to Bourg-en-Bresse further up north in the Alps area to finalize its organisation. It was composed of both infantry (800 men) and cavalry (200), both designated as chasseurs. Whereas in early 1793 the cavalry was sent to Fontainebleau in the Paris area, the infantry remained as part of the army of the Alps. It was then renamed légion des Alpes. Most of the men and officers came from the former 101e regiment (royal-liegeois, a former foreign unit) which had been disbanded for disciplinary reasons.

The law and decrees did not give any indication of its uniform and the one sketch by Victor, also copied by Marbot, shows an all light blue uniform with white piping with the exception of red lapels. Therefore, Boisselier's decision to give this man light blue lapels is odd and may be a copying mistake.

Apart from the uniform colour, this man is identical to regular chasseur units similar to the 17e bis and 18e bis chasseurs battalions in the army of the Alps.

Plate 25
1ère légion des francs 1796, Grenadier et Tambour
D'après les mémoires du général Bigarré, Striedbeck et la collection Boersch.[39]

This plate shows the earlier dress of the légion noire officially known as 1ère légion des francs, which we have presented and discussed for Plate 7. For Plate 7 the source was a contemporary watercolour done by an eyewitness during the campaign in Switzerland in 1799 when it had become the 14e légère demi-brigade. This plate uses Bigarré's memoirs as well as paper soldiers done by Boersch and Striedbeck, which are period sources. Striedbeck, an Alsatian from Strasburg just like Zix (who was Boersch's source), probably saw those men when they passed by Strasburg.

We have here a grenadier and a drummer. This latter figure being shown by Boersch. One can note the number of buttons on the grenadier's coat as well as the odd cuff lapels which do not cover the cuffs. The drummer is distinguished by white lace at its collar, cuffs and lapels and a tricolour plume.

It is in this dress that the unit embarked on its ill-fated attempt at invading Ireland which only resulted in a fight against British ships at sea and a shipwreck due to foul weather.

Plate 26
Légion Batave 1793 ou corps des chasseurs-tirailleurs bataves d'après des documents de l'époque, archives de Bréda.
Légion germanique, chasseur à pied 1792–1793 d'après l'ouvrage de Chuquet et le recueil de Lienhart et Humbert.[40]

Légion Batave 1793 ou corps des chasseurs-tirailleurs bataves
The Dutch Republic had long been a model for liberal intellectuals throughout Europe. Many philosophers and political opponents to autocratic monarchies had, throughout the seventeenth

---
39   1st Legion of the Franks 1796, grenadier and drummer. From the memoirs of General Bigarré, Striedbeck and the Boersch collection. Dated August 1943.
40   Dutch Legion 1793 or Dutch Tirailleurs-Chasseurs according to documents of the period, Bréda archives. Germanic Legion, foot chasseur 1792–1793 according to the work by Chuquet and the Lienhart and Humbert collection. Dated May 1943.

and first part of the eighteenth century taken refuge or published their works in Holland. However, the United Provinces had gradually transformed into a quasi-monarchy under the rule of the Orange family as the main executive role of Stadhouder had implicitly become hereditary.

Even before the onset of the French revolution, the Dutch had made their own attempt at a revolution, which had failed and thus the Dutch patriots had taken refuge in France, like the Belgians and later the Poles. They had formed a Batavian revolutionary committee. It negotiated with the French government the creation of a légion franche étrangère – a free foreign legion. This unit was to be composed only of non-French individuals but avoided being too obviously considered Dutch by using a neutral denomination. Yet, its administrative body was composed only of Dutchmen. It had both a catholic and a protestant priest and its initial location was Dunkirk where the Dutch revolutionaries had been regrouped. Like many legions of the period, it was a multi-branch unit grouping cavalry, infantry, and artillery.

The legion walked into Belgium with the French army and then participated in the invasion of Holland. After the defeat of Neerwinden, it retreated with the French army. As it had suffered heavy losses, it was disbanded in November 1793, its remaining men were transferred into the 13e chasseurs à cheval and the 30e légère demi-brigade.

The source given by Boisselier is indicated as 'archives of Breda'. As previously mentioned Boisselier probably used plate #7 from Band XVIII of Richard Knötel's *Uniformenkunde*. Knötel copied a contemporary manuscript found in the Breda archives showing Pichegru's troops which had taken Breda in 1794. One of the figures on the plate is labelled as 'légion Batave'.

The legion was also represented by another contemporary artist, by the name of Gregorius in more detail, including all its various branches. This work was copied by C.C.P Lawson and this version can be found in the Anne S.K. Brown Collection. Gregorius shows a plainer uniform but similar in colours and style to that given by the Breda manuscript. The sky-blue distinctive colour on collar, cuffs and lapels was a Dutch characteristic. Later Dutch units serving for the French kept that distinctive colour. The white stripes on the forearms may be an indication of an NCO rank, but we have no confirmation of that. The red piping for the waistcoat seems more to be an individual choice than regulation, likewise for the gaiters.

Légion germanique, chasseur à pied 1792–1793
The légion germanique is one of the most curious units raised in 1792–1793. Its history is also fairly well known as Arthur Chuquet, a late nineteenth and early twentieth century historian devoted a full volume to it, having used all the contemporary documentation which had survived.

It was raised in early September 1792 from German 'patriots'. Like the Dutch volunteer units, the revolution had attracted many German liberals who opposed their various native governments. It was supposed to be a fairly large body with a total of 3,000 men: 1,000 cavalry and 2000 infantry, as well as some artillery. The cavalry is discussed with the next plate.

The infantry was composed of chasseurs (two battalions) and arquebusiers (one battalion). The word arquebuse is actually usually used for the old matchlock gun, and seems to have been just adopted as a fancy name to designate the elite companies rather than the more common title of grenadiers.

Swiss guards who had avoided or survived the 10 August 1792 massacre at the Tuileries joined this unit, but also other Swiss from the former disbanded Swiss regiments. It also attracted Germans, Poles, Belgians and even some Italians, many having been part of the former foreign regiments. Its initial staff was composed of Prussians and Austrians and one Alsatian (Schauenbourg). Interestingly, Augereau, the future Napoleonic *maréchal* was an *adjudant-major* in it.

As with many such units hastily organised from various nationalities and units, it suffered a very high rate of desertion. It was initially to be sent to the Pyrenees, but when the insurrection in Vendee started, it was diverted to that area. Its force when arriving there was around 2,600 men – close to its original planned strength. It took a severe beating from the Royalist forces at Saumur on 9–10 June 1793. As many of the men had been part of the former royal army, they plundered the treasury chest of the unit and simply joined the royalists. There they formed the excellent German companies of the Royalist army. As a result, it was formally disbanded on 23 June 1793, nine months after its formation. What was left of the infantry went into the 22e bataillon de chasseurs.

To attract its men, the legion had a colourful uniform. Its dress was considered of excellent quality and appearance, and it was known as la belle légion germanique. The coat was green, in line with the chasseur tradition, but the collar was white, as were the epaulette straps. Lapels were red for the chasseurs, while black for the arquebusiers, cuffs were sky blue and cuff lapels red. Turnbacks were white for chasseurs and black for arquebusiers. Although Boisselier does not show it, chasseurs probably had white fringe epaulettes with red piping for the strap, while arquebusiers had black fringe epaulettes with a black strap. Waistcoat and breeches were buff. Boisselier shows short light infantry gaiters, while other sources give full infantry grey-black gaiters. As a headdress the chasseurs and arquebusiers had the ubiquitous 1791 helmet with a tricolour plume.

Plate 27
Piconnier de la légion germanique 1792–1794 Lienhart et Humbert et la légion germanique de Chuquet.[41]

The cavalry of the Légion germanique was its most innovative part. It had four squadrons of cuirassiers légers and four of piqueurs or piconniers (pikers). Of course, one can only wonder what a 'light cuirassier' actually was! The commander and founder of the legion, a Prussian by the name of Dambach actually boasted that 600 of his cuirassiers légers could overrun 3,000 enemy cavalry. As it turned out the cuirassiers légers were decimated at the Battle of Saumur, on 9 June 1793.

We do have a description for the cuirassiers légers as wearing a light articulated cuirass made of leather with metal epaulettes and a metal helmet. All this worn over a buff leather jerkin. Boisselier attempted a reconstruction which one can find in another series devoted to revolutionary troops which is in the Anne S.K. Brown Collection. It looks like a regular Napoleonic cuirassier but in buff with a leather cuirass. Actually, unless some contemporary image surfaces, which is unlikely, no one knows what they really looked like. Marceau the future general and hero of the Revolutionary Wars was a *lieutenant* in the cuirassiers légers.

The piconniers are easier to depict as they fundamentally wore the same uniform as the chasseurs à pied, with red turnbacks. They were armed with a light cavalry sabre and a 'pike' – the term was sometimes used at the time rather than lance. Boisselier gives a white tipped sky-blue plume, but other sources give black. Pikes were quite popular as a revolutionary weapon as they were fairly easy to mass produce.

---

41 Piker of the Germanic Legion 1792–1794. Lienhart and Humbert and Chuquet's book on the Germanic Legion. Dated August 1943.

Plate 28
Légion des Allobroges créée en 1792 dessin de Victor et collection A. de Marbot
Légion du Nord 1793 – document de l'époque, archives de Bréda.[42]

Légion des Allobroges 1792
The Allobroges was the name of a gallic tribe at the time of Caesar's conquest which was established in the Lyon-Savoy area. In the typical late eighteenth-century taste for the classics and antiquity, the name was adopted for a unit raised in that region.

Savoy was not then part of France but belonged to the kingdom of Piedmont-Sardinia whose ruling family was the house of Savoy. However, its inhabitants spoke French, or a dialect derived from French, and there were many 'patriots' in a similar fashion to Holland and Germany. During the summer of 1792, the legion was raised and planned to be a combined force of infantry, cavalry and artillery. A battalion of chasseurs à pied was indeed ready in time for the successful invasion of Savoy. After that, the legion recruited from the newly formed department of Mont-Blanc. By the spring of 1793, its cavalry was ready, and a review of the legion took place in Rumilly. The legion was then directed towards Marseilles and Toulon which had rebelled against the Republic to fight against both insurrections. It was actually the spearhead unit at both sieges. In early 1794, it was transferred to the eastern Pyrenees to fight against the Spanish. In June 1794 its cavalry was transferred to the 15e Dragons leaving only the infantry, which by 1795 was merged into the 4e légère demi-brigade which then joined the army of Italy. Compared to other legion units, the Allobroges had a much better battle record than most and was, by the time it became regular light infantry, considered an elite veteran unit.

Its uniform is rather well known through archival records but also, as indicated by Boisselier, from a sketch by Victor and a representation on a Marbot plate. The overall aspect is typical of light infantry or chasseurs, with an all green uniform with red lapels and piping on collar and pointed cuffs. The headdress shown is the 1791 helmet but when the Allobroges were formed most men actually only had felt hats.

Légion du Nord 1793
This légion du Nord was raised in Valenciennes, a town in the north of France in May and June of 1792. The future general Westermann was its *colonel* as of September 1792 and remained at its head despite being promoted to *général de brigade* in May 1793.

It participated in the invasion of Holland where it was seen at Breda and depicted in the manuscript already mentioned which provided the source for this plate. Afterwards it was sent to the Vendée where its infantry was annihilated when confronted by the Royalist forces. Its cavalry however participated in the final chase of the retreating Royalist forces known as the virée de Galerne (Galerne trek).

Boisselier's representation is based on the Breda manuscript as represented in Richard Knötel's plate which we have already mentioned. The uniform is entirely sky-blue with red collar, lapels, cuffs. The sky-blue breeches also have bastion shaped laces on each thigh. There is a profusion of yellow metal buttons on cuff lapels but also on those bastion laces, probably indicating either real

---

42 Allobroges Legion created in 1792, drawing by Victor and A. de Marbot collection. Northern Legion 1793 – period document, Bréda archives. Dated May 1943.

or simulated pockets. As usual the headdress is the 1791 helmet. Sadly, the uniform of the cavalry is not known to us.

Plate 29
Grenadier, légion des francs du Nord 1799 – Lienhart et Humbert – Marbot, Journal Militaire
Grenadier, légion du Danube 1799 d'après une estampe de l'époque de Rugendas.[43]

The evolution of the political situation at the end of the revolution resulted in the organisation of new legions which, as such, had only a relatively short existence. Yet they were much needed as the Republic was facing a resurgence of its main enemies and had lost, or risked losing, the territories it had previously gained.

Grenadier, légion des francs du Nord 1799
The légion des francs du Nord (legion of the northern franks) is in many ways a purely political creation with little actual military justification other than raising troops from an area which had now been securely in French hands for some time.

The left bank of the Rhine had been invaded in 1794 and united to France through an occupation administration. Multiple territories had been merged, some belonging to Prussia, and others which were independent. The local inhabitants had grown accustomed to the French presence and actually felt it made sense to become part of the French Republic, just as had happened with the former Austrian Netherlands (Belgium).

The raising of a local troop was decided upon on 8 September 1799, and it was aptly named légion des francs du Nord, implying the local population was as French as the rest of France.

Organised in Aachen, it actually could not muster many men and it ended up being, yet again a foreign legion with as many as 14 nationalities in its ranks! Although it was supposed to have cavalry, this never materialized and so, instead two legions of infantry were raised totalling eight battalions. In late 1800, it participated in Moreau's armée du Rhin as part of its left wing and was present at Hohenlinden (3 December 1800).

In 1801, it was part of Augereau's Gallo-Batavian army and therefore in Holland. The Batavian Republic was asked to provide for its support both financially and logistically. By then, the left bank of the Rhine had been incorporated into the French Republic. The legion was therefore disbanded, and its men were incorporated into regular units: the 55e ligne demi-brigade and 18e légère demi-brigade.

Its uniform is known thanks to the *Journal Militaire* and Marbot's plate. It was an all green uniform with red collar, pointed cuffs and red piping on lapels and turnbacks. The grenadier shown here has the usual grenadier red fringe epaulettes.

Grenadier, légion du Danube 1799
The légion du Danube is part of the complex history of Polish troops under French service during the Revolutionary and Napoleonic period. During the summer of 1799, as the tide was turning

---
43 Grenadier, Legion of the Northern Francs 1799 – Lienhart and Humbert – Marbot, Military Journal. Grenadier, Danube Legion 1799 after a period print by Rugendas. Dated October 1943.

against the Republic, fresh troops needed to be had and Polish prisoners of war seemed an easy fix to such a problem.

Thus, a second Polish legion was raised from Russian and Austrian prisoners of war of Polish origin. This was done in the Jura area in Besançon. To avoid confusion with the existing Polish legions in Italy, it was renamed the légion du Danube. The legion had infantry, cavalry, and artillery. The infantry was organised first and was already fighting in the spring of 1800. The entire legion was however ready for Hohenlinden where it distinguished itself.

After that it was transferred to Italy and it ended up being stationed in the kingdom of Etruria, which had been made out of a part of Tuscany. Ultimately its infantry became the 3e Polish demi-brigade.

Interestingly the man represented does not wear any uniform item showing a Polish influence. It is based on a well-known print by Rugendas showing primarily the cavalry of the legion (which wears a typical Polish uhlan uniform with shapskas and other such typical Polish items of dress) but also this infantryman. The young Albrecht Adam who saw Moreau's troops in person, and did some naïve sketches of them represented them as wearing a shapska and a short coat with blue lapels, and cuffs, all trimmed with red. The organisation decree stipulated that a short blue coat was to be worn with red collar, cuffs, lapels and piping, blue trousers with red piping and a bonnet polonaise (a shapska). It is probable that, after some months of campaigning, the infantry had been refitted with an entirely French uniform, which would explain the Rugendas print.

Plate 30
Légion Italique, fusilier 8/9/1799, dessin de Martinet, Marbot, Lami, Journal Militaire
½ brigade Helvétique 19/12/1798, Journal Militaire et dessin colorié contemporain.[44]

Légion Italique, fusilier, 8 September 1799
By late 1799, the Cisalpine Republic – in effect a client state of the French Republic – had been overrun by the Austrians who had annihilated Bonaparte's gains of the first Italian campaign of 1796–1797. One of the consequences was that Italians favourable to the French sought refuge in France. The Republic needed to raise new troops to fight back and many of these men were available and ready to join.

On the same day (8 September 1799) as the légion des francs du Nord and the légion du Danube were formally raised, the légion italique was organised. As the governmental decree of that day stated:

> …a great number of Italian patriots which have taken refuge in France, are eager to fight for the cause of liberty which they so generously embraced when the French entered Italy, and furthermore they have the most pressing interest to go back to their fatherland…the circumstances require that our armies be increased in size so we can push back the enemy and bring victory yet again under the flags of the French Republic.[45]

---

44 Italic Legion, fusilier 8/9/1799, drawing by Martinet, Marbot, Lami, Military Journal. Swiss demi-brigade 19/12/1798, Military Journal and contemporary coloured drawing. Dated November 1943.
45 Loi aui autorise la création d'une légion étrangère sous la dénomination d'Italique, du 22 fructidor an 7, *Journal Militaire de l'AN VII*, p.731.

The legion was to have four battalions of infantry each having a company of grenadiers, one of chasseurs à pied and eight of fusiliers, four squadrons of chasseurs à cheval and also a company of light artillery.

The uniform was the same for all branches, the difference being the wearing of short gaiters for infantry and short boots for cavalry and artillery. It was a very similar outfit to the one chosen for the légion des francs du Nord: all green but with a different distinctive colour. Collar, cuffs, turn-backs and pipping were yellow. Grenadiers and fusiliers wore a three cornered hat, basically the usual infantry hat, the rest, artillery, mounted and foot chasseurs wore a felt hat, which is shown on the next plate.

By 1800, given the number of additional men available as prisoners of war who were released by the Austrians, the legion increased in size adding a battalion of supernumerary officers and two companies of supernumerary NCOs. By 1800, the légion italique became the légion italienne and had a battalion of light infantry, two companies of artillery (one mounted, one foot), mounted chasseurs and hussars. It participated actively in the first phases of the second Italian campaign. After the victory at Marengo, the Cisalpine Republic was restored and the legion left French service, was disbanded (4 September 1800), and its different components were integrated into the new army of the Cisalpine Republic.

For this figure, Boisselier had many excellent sources. There is of course the organisation decree in the *Journal Militaire*, but also plates by both Marbot and Lami (published in 1821). His representation closely follows all of these. It is to be noted that the light infantry of the Italian Republic and later kingdom of Italy would match the colours of the légion italique.

Demi-brigade helvétique 19 December 1798

After 10 August 1792, the French Republic stopped employing Swiss troops. The only Swiss that remained in French service did so by joining various units on an individual and personal basis. The situation changed in 1798 when, under pressure from the victorious French, the Swiss agreed on 19 December 1798 to raise 18,000 men to join French service. The resulting exact number of men available probably did not reach that level. Six demi-brigades helvétiques were finally organised which were ultimately regrouped into three. These were the forerunners of the future Swiss regiments of the later Napoleonic armies. Until 1803, the Swiss wore their own national uniform and kept their national cockade.

This explains the rather odd combination of colours worn by this figure. The uniform was of typical French cut, as was the armament and equipment but the blue coat had yellow cuffs and lapels with red trimming, a red collar with yellow trimming and green cuff lapels trimmed red. The cockade shown by Boisselier is incorrect as the French cockade was worn only after 1803 – the correct one is also tricolour but with a green centre, and then red and yellow. A plume was also worn, the base being green then red and tip being yellow.

The Swiss demi-brigades fought in Massena's army in 1799 in Switzerland. The 1er, 2e, a part of the 4e, and the grouped grenadier companies of all of the demi-brigades fought at Zürich on 1 August 1799. After that and until the organisation of the new Swiss regiments, these demi-brigades were used for garrison duty.

Plate 31
Grenadier des bataillons auxiliaires 1799 créés le 14 Messidor An VII (2/7/1799)
Chasseur de la légion du Nord, 22 fructidor an VII Journal Militaire.[46]

Grenadier des bataillons auxiliaires 1799

> …the safety of the fatherland commands the legislative body to determine without any further delay the organisation of battalions and companies…conscripts…will be grouped into battalions in the departments where they reside…these auxiliary battalions will take the name of the departments where they are formed.[47]

On 2 July 1799, the French Republic ordered that all conscripts be formed into battalions as soon as possible. This meant that the battalions were formed in each department and then pressed into service. The situation was similar to that of 1792, except that there was no longer a formal need to call in volunteers as conscription had been set up. The law indicated that they were to be provided by the central administration with a uniform identical in fact to that of the infantry. Boisselier's figure is perfectly in line with that text used as its source.

Chasseur de la légion du Nord 1799
Like the légion italique the légion des francs du Nord, later the légion du Nord, was to have a felt hat with a plume for its chasseurs, mounted and foot, and for its light artillery. There is no other detail in the text in the *Journal Militaire*. Based on this Boisselier has reconstructed what a chasseur could have looked like. The felt hat is actually the early type of shako, which was becoming fashionable with light troops in 1799–1800, with a green plume on the side.

Plate 32
Légion Polonaise vers 1798, d'après Hoffmann
Légion de Dombrowsky d'après Victor.[48]

The full story of the Polish legions would require a volume of their own and so only a brief outline is given here.
　In 1795, Poland as an organised state was erased from the map of Europe and its territory divided between Austria, Prussia, and Russia. From that moment on and until 1918, the Polish question became a source of instability in Europe, as Poles fought to have an independent country once again.
　Many Poles had already taken refuge in Paris, even before the final disappearance of their country, and had lobbied for help. In 1792, Wojciech Turski had been sent as a deputy by a group of Polish patriots to the French legislative body. Under the name of Albert le Sarmate (Albert the Sarmatian) he wrote articles and petitions, and joined the French army in 1793.

---

[46] Grenadier of the auxiliary battalions 1799 created on 14 Messidor year 7 (2/7/1799) Chasseur of the Northern Legion, 22 Fructidor year 7, Military Journal. Dated November 1943.
[47] Loi relative à l'organisation des bataillons et des compagnies dont la formation est ordonnée par la loi du 10 Messidor an 7, du 14 Messidor an 7, *Journal Militaire An VII*, p.582.
[48] Polish Legion circa 1798, after Hoffmann. Dombrowsky Legion after Victor. Dated August 1943.

But when the French conquered the north of Italy, Polish patriots saw the opportunity raise units serving the French. Two legions were raised with Bonaparte's support but under the service of the Lombard Republic on 9 January 1797. Command was given to Henryk Dabrowski (pronounced Dombrowski). Although their participation in the campaign was fairly limited, the Polish legions quickly established themselves as reliable units. In 1799, still stationed in Italy, they fought against the Austrians.

When Boisselier painted this plate, contemporary knowledge of iconographic sources for the legions was fairly limited. There were the various gouaches done by Hoffmann, here used for the grenadier on the right, and one sketch by Victor used for the figure on the left.

Since then, two contemporary manuscripts have surfaced, the *Cronaca Rovatti* a chronicle written and illustrated by a cleric in Modena, and a similar such chronicle from Florence. Both show in detail the Polish legions: infantry, cavalry, and artillery. They also are closer in aspect to the Hoffmann paintings.

Victor's sketch may actually represent some later aspect and may have been observed outside of Italy. Both however show that the legions wore a short coat with square cut lapels, later to be known as a kurtka (a word which in Polish simply means coat or jacket) and had a specific Polish cap.

The cap was to become famous as the shapska and became quite popular not only with Polish troops but also with other units. This square cap is an evolution of the soft and loose peasant's cap as worn by the Polish insurgents in 1794. The Polish national cavalry wore a similar but more rigid type of cap. The Polish word czapka was transformed by the French into 'shapska'.

In both cases, Boisselier has been quite faithful to the original sources. The drawing by Victor seems to show that the tricolour belt doubled as a cartridge holder. Each loop of the belt being able to have one full musket cartridge.

The Polish legions' uniforms set the tone for the many future Polish units serving with the French and then later in the Duchy of Warsaw, a short-lived attempt at reviving a Polish state.

Plate 33
Chasseurs de Paris 1794–1796
Legion de Westermann 1792–1794
d'après Victor, collection Dubois de l'Estang, musée de l'armée.[49]

Chasseur de Paris 1794–1796
Paris, the cradle and hotbed of the revolution, had to distinguish itself by raising multiple volunteer units to display it ardent patriotism. In fact, the number of units raised is rather bewildering. Many were quite simply volunteers from the Garde nationale sections and wore their regular uniforms. Others adopted a different dress to distinguish themselves or simply because they faced logistical constraints. There are actually very few documents which detail what was worn. The contemporary iconographic sources which have survived, such as Victor's sketches show figures with fairly generic unit names, such as in this case – chasseur de Paris. Multiple units claimed such a title.

---

49 Paris Chasseurs 1794–1796. Westermann Legion 1792–1794 after Victor, Dubois de l'Estang collection, Army Museum. Dated August 1943.

In fact, this man belonged to one of the four companies raised in the Louvre district and otherwise known as Chasseurs du Louvre. All served on the eastern border where they were quite active, except for the second which was sent to the armée des Pyrénées occidentales.

The uniform chosen is a copy of the regulation line chasseurs à pied uniform and actually quite similar to that of the 10e bataillon. Boisselier copied the Victor sketch. Text sources mention that the lapels were trimmed with red, and that the waistcoat was to be white, instead of the buff shown here.

Legion de Westermann 1792-1794
We have actually already discussed this unit with plate 28 under the name of légion du Nord, but it was also known as Legion de Westermann, after its commander. This here is a very different type of uniform compared to the one known through the Breda manuscript. The source is a sketch by Victor reproduced also in a plate by Marbot.

Was this the very first uniform adopted by the unit, which later took on the 1791 helmet? Or is this rather the dress worn by the chasseurs in the unit, which would explain the distinctive light troops features such as a Corsican or Tyrolean style hat with a green and white plume, but also the green collar and pointed cuffs? This is the option we tend to favour, but there are no formal textual sources available to confirm it.

Plate 34
Légion de Paris 1793-1794, d'après Victor, collection Dubois de l'Estang Musée de l'armée Compagnies Franches 1792, d'après Valmont, bibliothèque nationale.[50]

Légion de Paris 1793-1794
This unit was known under multiple names: the 1ère compagnie franche de chasseurs de Paris, the légion de Paris, and the légion de Dutruy.

It was organised in July 1792 by a former dragoon trooper by the name of Joseph Burg. His father was rich enough to have properly dressed and equipped the unit. At the end of August, it was sent to the eastern borders. In October Burg was replaced by Dutruy, a former Swiss soldier from the Vigier regiment. It was under the name of légion de Dutruy that the unit was better known. It was quite active during the end of 1792 and Dutruy was authorized to increase the unit strength by incorporating men from other volunteer units but also enemy deserters; German, Swiss and others. As a result, Dutruy's legion was quickly known as a band of rogue soldiers known for looting the towns where they were stationed. It became the 15e légère bataillon d'infanterie in January 1793 and ultimately in May changed its numbering to 19e. By which time Dutruy had been promoted to *général de brigade*.

Again, the source is a sketch by Victor but also a plate by Marbot; both show this odd very Austrian looking uniform. It is quite probable that such dress was adopted using captured stores, but we have no contemporary evidence for this.

---

50   Paris Legion 1793-1794, after Victor, Dubois de l'Estang collection, Army Museum. Free Light Companies 1792, after Valmont, National Library. Dated August 1943.

Compagnies Franches 1792
The adjective franc or franche designates light volunteer troops. This figure is taken from a watercolour by Valmont, who also shows other units taken from Marbot's plates. Valmont does not mention any source, and this is therefore a fairly generic type. The man wears an overall light grey infantry style uniform with a 1791 helmet. Valmont actually gives him a white waistcoat. This is in fact a possible uniform for volunteer units raised as an emergency given the war situation and using grey cloth which was available cheaply and in quantity.

Plate 35

Compagnies Franches Basques 1793, bataillons de chasseurs basques
(les chasseurs basques du citoyen Labouche, dessin de Lacauchie et aquarelle de la bibliotèque nationale, estampes).[51]

Although traditionally much emphasis is given to the eastern and northern front, the southern front and more specifically the Pyrenees border was also under pressure during 1792 and 1793. The King of Spain was, after all, a cousin of King Louis XVI, and since the early eighteen century when the Bourbon dynasty had started reigning over Spain, the country had become a traditional ally of France, fighting at its side during the American Revolution.

As of October 1792, several companies of Basque volunteers were raised in the Basque country at the extreme west end of the Pyrenees. The men wore, as shown on this plate, the typical local civilian costume including the large beret which could be of various bright colours, but more usually red as shown here. Such a dress was to be used yet again later in 1813–1814 for volunteer units.

By December 1793, the Basques had raised enough men for four battalions. In June 1793, it had been determined that this dress was inadequate for 'either the citizens or the type of war'.[52] Probably worried at the lack of uniformity and the too obvious local specificities, the governmental representatives asked that a regular light infantry uniform be adopted. This is actually what Boisselier has shown for the second figure which is a chasseur from the Basque battalions in late 1793–1794.

Plate 36

Légions franches de l'Ouest – carabinier et chasseurs à cheval, décret du 3e jour complémentaire an VII (19 septembre 1799) Journal Militaire.[53]

In 1799, the French Republic was faced not only with renewed and successful attacks from its external enemies such as Austria and Russia, but also had to cope with internal foes. In the west, the Royalist insurrection was active again and as the law passed on the 19 September 1799 clearly

---

51 Basque Free Light Companies 1793, Basque Chasseur battalions (citizen Labouche's Basque Chasseurs, drawing by Lacauchie and watercolour from the National Library, prints). Dated July 1943.
52 Arrêté des représentants en mission à l'armée des Pyrénées Occidentales, 6 June 1793 – quoted in Didier Davin, 'Corps francs et compagnies franches de la révolution (1792-1799)', *SEHRI* blog, < https://sehrileblog.wordpress.com/2017/03/07/corps-francs-et-compagnies-franches-de-la-revolution-1792-1799-1ere-partie/>, accessed 30 April 2024.
53 Free Legions of the West – carabinier and mounted chasseur, decree of the 3rd supplementary day of year 7 (19th September 1799) Military Journal. Dated November 1943.

stated: '…considering the number and audacity of the "chouans" which increases daily in the west, that it is urgent to stop their destructions, their progress against liberty, to safeguard republicans and bring these together under the flags of liberty…' It was decreed that a légion franche would be raised in each department of the west. Each was to be composed of a battalion of light infantry (eight companies – one of carabiniers, one of sappers, six of fusiliers) and a mounted chasseurs company. The uniform for the infantry was that of the light infantry, for the sappers they were to wear what their regular counterparts wore in the army. Only the mounted chasseurs had a uniform and equipment spelt out in detail by the regulations, namely a 'Short green jacket, with scarlet collar, cuffs and waistcoat, white piping and buttons, similar piping on the waistcoat, with 3 rows of white and round buttons. Green pants with short boots and a felt cap with a tricolour plume. Horse equipment to be that of the mounted chasseurs. Scarlet sabretache with the name of the department in white.'[54]

This is effectively what Boisselier has shown with these two figures. The carabinier is identical to a carabinier of regular light infantry. The mounted chasseur is as per the text above with a sabretache on which it is written 'légion franche de la loire inf r' (free legion of the lower loire). One could argue that the text should have been only 'Loire Inférieure'.

Plate 37
Cavalier, 4e regiment de dragons vers 1794, collection Hennin
Trompette au 22e regiment de dragons, 1ère république, Collection Dubois de l'Estang.[55]

There were 18 dragoon regiments in 1791 and at the start of the war. Dragoons (dragons in French) were classified as light cavalry. The bulk of the French cavalry was provided by the régiments de cavalerie. Alongside these were dragoons, some hussar regiments, and the newly formed chasseurs à cheval.

Dragoons had existed since the time of Louis XIV and were initially mounted infantry. Indeed, they were still trained both as cavalry and as infantry to some extent. Their specific training, equipment, and medium-sized horses made them the most flexible cavalry force in the French army, and they were extensively used for both reconnaissance and battle in all theatres during the Revolutionary War. By contrast the régiments de cavalerie with their heavier mounts were better suited to the northern and eastern fields and pitched battles, to provide shock troops with a charge. Thus, dragoons were the main mounted components for the armies both in Italy and Egypt.

The Hennin collection being a very large set of iconographies covering all of French history, it is difficult to trace back which specific image was used as a source by Boisselier. He dates this figure from around 1794 but it actually could be any date between 1791–1799. The 4e regiment de dragons had scarlet as its distinctive colour and wore it at the collar, cuffs, lapels and turnbacks.

The trumpeter is indicated as taken from the Dubois de l'Estang collection – again it is difficult to trace back the source. It is probably one of those anonymous pen and ink sketches which are in bound volumes. In any case it is stated as being from the 22e regiment and first Republic. In 1803,

---

54 Loi qui ordonne la création de légions françaises dans sept départements, du 3e jour complémentaire an 7, *Journal militaire*, an VII, p.824.
55 Trooper, 4th Regiment of Dragoons, circa 1794, Hennin collection. Trumpeter, 22nd Regiment of Dragoons, 1st Republic, Dubois de l'Estang collection. Dated November 1943.

the dragoon sub-branch of cavalry was massively increased. In 1793, the number of regiments had been brought to 21 by transforming a number of volunteer units into regular dragoon regiments. On 24 September 1803, the cavalry regiments 13e to 18e became the 22e to 27e dragoons while the 7e bis, 11e and 12e hussars became the 28e, 29e and 30e dragoons. This clearly shows how popular the dragoons had become, providing a flexible cavalry force.

Therefore, this figure can only be dated to around 1803–1804, which is still, technically the Republic, although under the quasi exclusive leadership of Bonaparte as First Consul.

The distinctive colour taken by regiments 19 to 24 was daffodil, or a light yellow, which is totally absent from this figure. However, the 13e régiment de cavalerie had crimson as a distinctive colour. It is therefore possible that its trumpeters had this striking white coat with crimson collar, lapels, turnbacks and cuffs, and that it was kept after they transformed into dragoons. Also, one notes the gold/yellow lace mixed with scarlet which has replaced the Orleans lace which was used under the monarchy. As another distinction, the dragoon helmet has a scarlet flowing crest (instead of black) and a red plume.

Plate 38
Chef de demi-brigade de bataille 1792–1794, d'apres le recueil de Valmont.[56]

This is a direct copy of a fine watercolour done by Valmont. Although as usual he does not give his source, we can find similar figures in contemporary prints.

The *chef de demi-brigade* was the equivalent of the former regimental *colonel*. Our man has indeed the large golden epaulettes corresponding to this rank. Officers during the revolution and Napoleonic period did not necessarily ride horses. The more senior ranks: battalion commanders, *majors* and *colonels* normally did, but if too few mounts were available and they were needed for the cavalry and artillery, they would end up on foot with the one exception being the *colonel*.

The horse equipment is limited to grey and brown horse blankets thrown over the saddle. The most striking part of the figure is his 1791 helmet which has a crest shorter in the front than usual and with a tail at the back. Again, such an oddity can be observed in contemporary iconography. Finally, he sports a tricolour plume, typical of the period and indicative of him being part of the regimental staff, indeed being the commanding officer.

Plate 39
Tambour de carabiniers à la 1ère demi-brigade légère vers 1798 collection Boersch
Trompette de grosse cavalerie, 1ère république, collection Dubois de l'Estang.[57]

This plate combines two very different figures from two very different sources.

Tambour de carabiniers à la 1ère demi-brigade légère vers 1798
This drummer is copied on a set of paper soldiers done by Boersch probably between 1812 and the 1820s. Boersch was a baker in Strasburg, and he had seen multiple units come by his town

---

56 Commanding officer, line demi-brigade 1792–1794. After the Valmont collection. Dated December 1943.
57 Carabinier drummer of the 1st light demi-brigade, circa 1798, Boersch collection. Heavy cavalry trumpeter, 1st Republic, Dubois de l'Estang collection. Dated November 1943.

and probably his bakery. He was also the nephew of the artist Benjamin Zix who had followed the Revolutionary and Napoleonic armies as an official artist working for Vivant Denon. Tradition states that Boersch inherited Zix's documentation and used it extensively. This makes the Boersch paper soldiers quite valuable as a primary source, even for the earlier revolutionary period.

In this case, this figure is dated at around 1798 when forces were stationed in the Rhine area. The distinctive purple-crimson lapels, collar and cuff lapels are confirmed for the 1er légère by other local paper soldier collections. The design of the tricolour lace is featured on several sources and was used well into the Empire. The hanging scarlet plume on the bearskin is typical of the revolutionary period. In conclusion this seems like and accurate representation of a carabinier drummer of the 1er légère towards the end of the revolutionary period.

Trompette de grosse cavalerie, 1ère république
Like the previous 22e dragons trumpeter (see plate 37) this figure comes from the extensive Dubois de l'Estang collection and there are no other indications as to which cavalry unit he belongs. Assuming he wears reversed colours for his coat, it is probable that he belongs to one of the first six regiments that had scarlet as a distinctive colour. The simple plain white lace (and epaulettes) has replaced any previous royal lace. The trumpet banner looks fairly elaborate and such style points to the late revolutionary period after 1796 and even the consular period.

Plate 40
Gendarmerie nationale 1796 d'après une estampe du temps, cabinet des estampes
Carabinier 1794 d'après le recueil de Leo à Leipzig.[58]

Despite a somewhat similar looking uniform, these two figures have nothing in common!

Gendarmerie nationale 1796 d'après une estampe du temps, cabinet des estampes
Under the monarchy and prior to 1791, the police force in France was the maréchaussée, which was composed of multiple units, somewhat independent and reporting to local provincial administrations.

In 1791, the maréchaussée as such disappeared and instead a homogeneous military force was organised; the gendarmerie nationale. The word gendarmerie comes from gens d'armes (men at arms) and was previously reserved to the elite cavalry units which were part of the royal household that had been disbanded.

The new gendarmerie was a force tasked with policing duties, especially in the countryside, but could also operate as regular cavalry if needed. The gendarmerie nationale has survived to this day and remains the regular police force outside of the larger French towns where the national or local police is in charge. Although still technically a military force, it now is part of the Ministère de l'Intérieur along with all other national police forces.

During the revolution, the new gendarmerie had much to do, outside of chasing petty criminals and thieves. It was active against the various insurrections, especially in the Vendée. It was also active against large criminal bands which raided the countryside taking advantage of the

---

58 National Gendarmerie 1796 from an early print, print room. Carabinier 1794 from Leo's collection in Leipzig. Dated December 1943.

confused situations caused by the revolution, and of course, they were tasked with going after runaway conscripts. The blue and red coat along with the large bicorn hat with white lace would remain specific to the gendarmerie throughout the nineteenth century and become a familiar sight throughout France.

The gendarmerie displayed the three national colours: blue for the coat, red for its distinctive colour visible at collar, lapels, cuffs and turnbacks, white at the buttons, lapels cuffs and collar piping but also the red and white aiguillette which proved that the gendarmerie had an elite status. Waistcoat and breeches were buff. Later this was also the case for the cartridge belt which became buff trimmed with white.

In terms of armament, the gendarmes had a straight sabre, similar to that worn by the dragoons sometimes with a grenade symbol (the grenade remains to this day the symbol of the gendarmerie). Gendarmes also carried very short flintlock pistols which could be tucked in their coat pockets. Such pistols had been already designed for the maréchaussée and continued to be in use for the gendarmerie and updated regularly with every new armament system which was regulated. Such weapons were often also carried by infantry officers who found them handy. Finally, short muskets (musketoons) were also provided – typically the heavy cavalry musket which was reinstated in the An IX system.

Boisselier has shown a typical gendarme using one of the numerous contemporary prints which showed such men.

Carabinier 1794 d'après le recueil de Leo à Leipzig
Technically, the two regiments of carabiniers were considered the elite of the cavalry and known as the grenadiers of the cavalry. They were under the command of the count of Provence (the future Louis XVIII). When all the army regiments abandoned names and took to numbering, the carabiniers became the 1er and 2e carabiniers and took rank prior to any other cavalry unit in the army order of battle. The carabiniers were quite conscious of their elite status and were always looked upon as an aristocratic body, both under the revolution and then the Empire. Because of this, there was known friction between them and the later Consular and Imperial Guard.

The carabiniers contributed to the revolutionary armies but exclusively on the eastern, or German, theatre of war where such a heavy body of cavalry would be effective with mass charges. A contemporary print by Rugendas of the Battle of Hohenlinden shows them at the forefront.

Their uniform was quite distinctive, as they carried the royal colours of red, white, and blue (Same as the future national colours). They had a medium sized bearskin with no plate, buff trimmed white leather equipment and carried specific sabres with a grenade at the hilt.

If this was the regulation uniform, it seems that, in the early stages of the Revolutionary Wars, a slightly different aspect could be observed. Boisselier's figure is based on a contemporary print by Leo, published in Leipzig, and which has provided already several types for this series.

Although given the title of a 'grenadier à cheval' it does show what is probably a carabinier. He has a regular carabinier coat but with white turnbacks, white cartridge belt and a medium-sized musket (as a carabinier would have). The strangest part is of course the bearskin. It has a white metal plate, which is somewhat logical as carabiniers had white metal buttons but also a tricolour plume (shown here as red and white), red and white cords, and what seems to be a small white metal grenade on the side. This might have been an interim headdress to display the carabiniers' attachment to the Republic as the plate shows Republican symbols. Later on, the contemporary iconography, such as Rugendas' plates, we have for the carabiniers is in line with their previous traditional look.

Plate 41

8e régiment de cavalerie ou régiment de cuirassiers 1792–1800
Ex. Cuirassiers du Roi: Hoffmann, W.Kobell, collection Dubois de l'Estang.[59]

The 8e régiment de cavalerie was an anomaly compared to all the other cavalry regiments. Known as the cuirassiers du Roi, it was the only regiment prior to 1792 which was armoured, wearing a full cuirass. Its distinctive colour was daffodil, a light yellow. It served throughout the period on the northern and eastern theatres of operation, including German lands. Given its unique look it was represented multiple times. Boisselier used many sources for this figure: Hoffmann of course which showed it in his series devoted to the 1786 regulation but more interestingly Kobell which shows in a wonderful and well-known coloured print an 8e cavalerie trooper in Germany in the later part of the period.

The 8e's unique equipment was imitated by other units as it became quickly obvious when confronted with Austrian cuirassiers that the lack of armour penalized French cavalry. In 1792, the first four cavalry regiments adopted armour. In 1804, the first 12 regiments of cavalry were formally transformed into cuirassiers. The other cavalry regiments, the 13e to the 18e became dragoons as indicated in the previous plate.

Plate 42

Cavalier au 2e régiment de cavalerie 1793, d'après un dessin de l'époque execute à Breda
Cavalier au 19e régiment de cavalerie 1795, d'après des documents contemporains de Holande et d'Allemagne.[60]

In 1792 when the war broke out, there were 24 regular cavalry regiments. On 21 February 1793, regiments 25e to 29e were added, but on 4 June 1793 the 15e regiment, the former Royal Allemand, a foreign regiment notoriously known for its Royalist sympathies, emigrated and so the total was down to 28 regiments. On 9 September 1799, the cavalry was brought down to 25 regiments. In 1803 only the first 12 regiments were kept and transformed into cuirassiers, regiments 13 to 18 became dragoons while the rest were disbanded and men transferred to various mounted units.

The heavy cavalry gradually evolved given the new tactical situation faced by the French army during the Revolutionary Wars. There was a need for light mounted units able to perform reconnaissance duty or practice la petite guerre (guerrilla warfare). For this, hussars, chasseurs and even dragoons were better suited than the heavy cavalry which had bigger horses and taller men.

The cavalry was dressed in a fashion similar to the infantry – a French style coat with long tails, but royal blue (later national blue) instead of white with a complex combination of the distinctive colour between collar, lapels, cuffs and cuff lapels. The initial 24 regiments were grouped in four sets of six, the first set having scarlet as its distinctive colour, the second daffodil, the third crimson, the fourth, pink. The regiments which were added in 1793 adopted the aurore (dawn) colour, a light orange. The distinctive colour was always in full on lapels and turnbacks, but for the

---

59 8th Cavalry Regiment or Cuirassiers Regiment 1792–1800. Formerly the King's Cuirassiers: Hoffmann, W.Kobell, Dubois de l'Estang collection. Dated December 1943.
60 Trooper from the 2nd Cavalry Regiment 1793, based on a contemporary drawing executed in Breda. Trooper from the 19th Cavalry Regiment 1795, based on contemporary documents from Holland and Germany. Dated October 1943.

rest its application would vary. Here for the 2e regiment, the collar is blue as are the cuff lapels, but the cuffs are scarlet (although they are not visible given the riding gloves).

The headdress was the regular infantry hat, under which the trooper would have some form of metal skull protection to protect from sabre cuts and thrusts. The plume would be black for two-thirds with the remaining third at the tip being of the distinctive colour.

The 2e cavalerie trooper shown by Boisselier and taken from the Breda manuscript, already mentioned in previous plates, is absolutely in line with the regulation.

The trooper from the 19e cavalerie is also dressed according to regulations. The one difference is that he has grey riding overalls reinforced with black leather worn over his riding boots.

Plate 43
Trompette de grosse cavalerie 1794 d'après le manuscrit de la collection Mellinet, cabinet des estampes, bibliothèque nationale.
Canonnier de l'artillerie à cheval 1792–1795 Journal Militaire et recueil A. de Marbot.[61]

Trompette de grosse cavalerie 1794
This figure is taken from the series of beautiful contemporary watercolours done by Hauck in Holland in 1794 and now in the Bibliothèque nationale de France. He wears a civilian dress which has been militarised. One can assume that he belongs to a cavalry regiment given his hat and overall look, but no specific regiment can be deduced.

He wears a dark blue open jacket with no distinctive colour at collar or cuffs. His waistcoat is also quite plain. Both these items are civilian sourced. Likewise for the red riding overalls with brown leather reinforcements. He has militarised his look by having a tricolour fringe epaulette on his right shoulder and simpler one on his left shoulder but with a tricolour aiguillettes. Finally, he has a tricolour plume on top of his hat. These tricolour symbols made him stand out amongst his unit which is what a trumpeter needed in the heat of battle.

Canonnier de l'artillerie à cheval 1792–1795 Journal Militaire et recueil A. de Marbot
It is on 29 April 1792, that the flying artillery or horse artillery came into existence. Horse artillery had existed in other countries and some experiments had been made in France prior to the revolution. The new, lighter carriages and guns in the Gribeauval gun system allowed for such a type of unit. In fact, the speed at which horse artillery would now be able to move on the battlefield would prove a major tactical evolution and a marked advantage for the French army.

At the start in 1792, as shown here by Boisselier, the uniform was identical to that of the foot gunners with the exception of the Hungarian style breeches and boots. Over time this hussar style would be reinforced and horse artillery would systematically copy the fanciful and extravagant dress enjoyed by the hussars and chasseurs.

The 1791 helmet provided some adequate protection for the riding artillerymen, but we know from other contemporary iconography that dragoon style helmets in leather or brass were also worn. Similarly, the type of headdress worn by chasseurs and hussars became quite popular over

---

61 Heavy cavalry trumpeter 1794 from a manuscript of the Mellinet collection, print room, National Library. Horse artillery gunner, 1792–1795 Military Journal and the A. de Marbot collection. Dated October 1943.

time. By the end of the revolution, the slightly conical mirliton cap or the early shako were worn by all mounted artillerymen.

Plate 44
Officier de chasseurs à cheval vers 1794 d'après le recueil contemporain de Léo
Cavalier au 5e regiment de chasseurs à cheval 1792, d'après l'affiche de recrutement du corps.[62]

Chasseurs à cheval were a new sub-branch of the cavalry. They had originally existed as part of the chasseur legions, and it was only in 1786 that they had become independent regiments.

At the outbreak of the war there were 12 chasseur regiments. Their uniform was somewhat of a simplified hussar dress: all green, a braided dolman and Hungarian breeches. White was the button colour which would also be used for braiding, and lace. Unlike the hussars they had no sabretache, no fancy pelisse, and wore the 1791 ubiquitous infantry helmet.

That is the figure represented on the right by Boisselier, a chasseur of the 5e (daffodil yellow as distinctive colour) taken from a recruitment poster. He is strictly as per regulations, down to the black plume tipped with the yellow distinctive colour. However, this regulation dress was often not followed – over time officers would adopt pelisse, sabretache and actually look like full hussars, but in green.

From a campaigning standpoint, the dolman with its braiding was not always the easiest piece of uniform to take care of. So, it is not surprising that the figure on the left taken from the series by Leo published in Leipzig in 1794, wears a French style coat with red piping. His Hungarian breeches also sport a tricolour V braiding. With time such a style would become the norm amongst chasseurs who gradually abandoned the hussar look after 1800, dolman and all, to adopt plainer dress similar to the one evident on this figure.

Plate 45
Chasseur à cheval vers 1798 d'après une estampe de Steinlen
Chasseur à cheval du 9e regiment 1795–1798 d'après une estampe de la bibliothèque nationale.[63]

In line with the comments made in the previous plate, these two chasseurs have adopted a green French-style coat, plainer and more comfortable to wear. The one on the left has the popular riding overalls with leather reinforcements. He wears a mirliton style cap with a tricolour plume. The distinctive colour seems to be scarlet worn at collar and cuffs, so he probably belongs to the 1er chasseurs.

The man on the right is copied from a watercolour by Raffet's son, itself a copy from a period document. It is clearly labelled as being the 9e chasseurs – but this would imply pink as a distinctive colour. This being said pink cloth was often quite dark and the distinction is only shown on the piping and collar. Our man wears an elegant red waistcoat, and he has an impressive cravat around

---

62 Officer of the mounted chasseurs circa 1794 from the contemporary Leo collection. Trooper from the 5th Regiment of Mounted Chasseurs 1792, from the recruitment poster of the unit. Dated October 1943.
63 Mounted chasseur circa 1798 after a print by Steinlen. Mounted chasseur of the 9th Regiment 1795-1798 after a print in the National Library. Dated December 1943.

his neck. He has a 1791 helmet but with a dropping horse mane at the back. Indeed, his style is more reminiscent of the later 1790s than the earlier periods.

Plate 46
Hussards de la liberté 1792 – capitaine
D'après Hoffmann et recueil de Marbot.[64]

The following plates illustrate various hussar-style volunteer units which in many cases ultimately merged and formed new regular hussar regiments. Raised at the same time as the volunteer legions in the emergency of the summer and fall of 1792, these troops ranged from acceptable to simply bad. The officers which organised them or were tasked to do so quite often did not have the relevant experience at best, and at worst were actually taking financial advantage of the situation getting money from the government and not actually fulfilling their role.

The hussards de la liberté were a flamboyant looking unit and are shown by Boisselier both on this plate and the following one. For this one, the first, a *capitaine* and on the next, a hussar trooper. They started as a fairly useless unit despite their elegant and original dress, but did in the end contribute to the creation of an iconic hussar regiment of the revolution, the 7e bis.

They were organized in Saint-Germain-en-Laye in the west of Paris on 2 September 1792 by *Général de brigade* Leygonnier with as its commander, citizen Ruttau. They were sent to the east. By the beginning of 1793, both war commissaries and representatives of the government concluded that funds had been wasted, recruitment was poor, and that barely one squadron was operational. By February 1793, it could muster 166 troopers but had only 135 sabres to arm them and no firearms! Rutau was dismissed and on 26 June 1793 the hussards de la liberté merged into the 7e bis hussars.

Nicolas Hoffmann, who was present during the revolution in Paris, devoted a series of plates entitled 'hussars according to the 1791 regulation and other new units even under the republic'. This volume was in the Tuileries palace library and disappeared in 1871 when the building was burned down during the Paris Commune. Margerand attempted its reconstruction in 1907 using notes that had been made by Vanson who had had access to it under the Second Empire. Marbot also had used that source, so his plates which shows this unit can also be used as a valid source. In the end Margerand managed to reconstruct 28 plates and published them.

The organisational decree gives no indication of the dress, so all we know really comes from Hoffmann who most probably saw them as they were in the Paris area. Although called hussars, their dress was not that of traditional hussars with dolman, pelisse, and sabretache. Two items were distinctive and original, the busy and the coat: the small sized busby displayed a red plume and bag. Such fur cap was identified with elite units, and this is probably why it was adopted to attract recruits. The coat was the oddest part. Cut like a traditional French-style blue coat with long tails, it did not have lapels but instead had hussar style braiding on the front but also on its rear pockets and cuffs. It also had a low flat turned down red collar somewhat out of fashion for the 1790s.

The rest was much more in line with hussar fashion, being a red braided waistcoat, Hungarian breeches, and boots. Officers had their rank displayed via the pointed lace pattern on the breeches but also with silver epaulettes on the coat, most certainly not a hussar habit!

---

64   Liberty Hussars 1792 – Captain. After Hoffmann and Marbot's collection. Dated July 1943.

Margerand clearly indicated, based on Vanson's notes, that the number 7 was visible on the trooper's saddle bag – therefore implying that they continued to wear this uniform when the 7e bis was initially created.

Plate 47
Hussard de la liberté, 1er corps, cavalier 1792 d'après Hoffmann
Chasseur à cheval de la légion franche étrangère 1793 d'après un document contemporain de Breda.[65]

The hussar has been discussed in the previous plate and there is not much more to add except that Boisselier gives him a laced clover style epaulette which Margerand did not show.

The second figure is a chasseur à cheval de la légion franche étrangère in 1793 taken from the Breda manuscript already mentioned in previous discussions of the plates.

We have seen that this legion, otherwise known as the Batavian legion, was composed of Dutch patriots and participated in the invasion of Holland in 1793. It was seen in Breda, and it was also reproduced by Richard Knötel in his *Uniformenkunde* plates. Another source for it are the watercolours by Gregorius of which we have excellent copies by Lawson currently in the Anne S.K. Brown Collection in the United States.

Both show a French style infantry coat with a red distinctive colour in the case of the Breda source and a dark pink for Gregorius (which could simply be a washed out red). The Breda document has epaulettes which could indicate the elite company. The Gregorius watercolour shows a 1791 helmet while Breda has a brass dragoon style helmet which might have been procured from army stores. In fact, the Breda chasseur looks more like a regular dragoon. As with the rest of the legion, it was almost annihilated and what was left of the cavalry was transferred into the 13e chasseurs.

Plate 48
Sous-officier au régiment des hussards volontaires de Jemmapes ou de la mort 1792–1793 – collection Boersch, Marbot, Lami et Martinet – deviant 10e hussards.[66]

This was probably one of the best known and most iconic units in the revolutionary armies. One of the reasons is that its striking uniform ensured it was represented by multiple artists. Boisselier indicated multiple sources for this plate: Boersch's Alsatian paper soldiers, Marbot but also Lami. There are quite a few more he could have indicated, including Margerand's reconstruction of Hoffmann plates mentioned before.

On 12 June 1792, in Paris two companies of hussars were raised with young volunteers ready to finance their uniform and equipment with their own funds. As a gesture of defiance to the threat to Paris caused by the Prussian army and its commander, the Duke of Brunswick, the new unit called

---

65 Liberty Hussars, 1st corps, trooper 1792 after Hoffmann. Mounted Chasseur Free Foreign Legion 1793 after a contemporary document from Breda. Dated July 1943.
66 Non-commissioned officer in the Jemmapes volunteer hussars regiment, or Death Hussars, 1792–1793 – Boersch, Marbot, Lami and Martinet collection – later 10th Hussars. Dated June 1943.

itself hussards de la mort (Death hussars) and on 28 July 1792 adopted the skull and crossbones of the Prussian Husaren-Regiment Nr. 5, along with a black uniform, laced and braided white.

As such, they existed only until 5 March 1793 when they were merged with other units to form the 13e chasseurs à cheval which ultimately became the 14e. However, the designation of hussards de la mort seemed to have been kept by the new 14e chasseurs and known throughout the army and by their enemies. In the Vendée, the 14e chasseurs acquired the reputation of a merciless unit spreading death and devastation throughout the countryside and was known as the death hussars, living up to their name. Coignet, much later during the Marengo campaign still referred to the 14e chasseurs as the death hussars.

The skull and crossbones symbol was displayed on the sabretache, and pelisse sleeves. This is confirmed by the multiple iconographic sources we have. Boisselier indicated in his caption that these hussars became the 10e hussars which is actually a mistake caused by the confusion between the hussards de la mort and the hussards noirs (black hussars) a volunteer unit raised by Dumouriez and which operated in the north.

Plate 49
Hussard de la Montagne 1793 6 Novembre
Hussard des Alpes 1792
D'après le recueil de Lienhart et Humbert.[67]

Hussard de la Montagne 1793
The armée des Pyrénées occidentales based at the most southwestern tip of France was facing Spain with little to no cavalry. On 6 November 1793, in Bayonne, a light cavalry squadron was raised from volunteers. It used small-sized mounts which they had in ample quantity, and which were otherwise useless for service in other theatres of war but well adapted to the local mountainous and rugged terrain of that region. The unit was named hussards de la montagne (hussars of the mountain) and by early 1794, a second squadron was in place at Orthez. In February 1794, it became the 12e hussards with three squadrons. A fourth and then a fifth and sixth squadron were raised. The 12e hussards fought with the armée des Pyrénées orientales against Spain, and afterwards was sent to the armée de l'Ouest.

Boisselier indicates that his source is the Lienhart and Humbert volume which is a late nineteenth century encyclopaedia on French uniforms. There are other more contemporary sources such as a portrait of *général de division* Servan with a hussar in the background, as well as Margerand's reconstruction of the 12e hussards. Margerand gives an entirely brown uniform with white braiding while Servan's portrait shows a hussar with an all brown uniform with yellow braiding, sky blue cuffs (and probably collar) and a mirliton cap with brown and sky blue flame.

It seems that the unit adopted a uniform based on that of the Chamborand hussars (2e). Both dolman and pelisse were brown. The breeches seemed to have been brown but also sky blue. As for braiding and buttons, they seemed to have been either white or yellow.

---

67 Mountain Hussars 1793 6 November. Alpine Hussars 1792. After the Lienhart and Humbert collection. Dated July 1943.

Hussard des Alpes 1792
The hussard des Alpes were raised only in January 1795 as part of the armée des Alpes, using various cavalry troops including the guides of that army. They existed as such only until September 1795 when they became the 13e hussards.

Again, the Lienhart & Humbert volumes are the source but we also have the Marbot plate and Margerand's reconstruction. They all agree on the uniform and Boisselier has reproduced it accordingly. This is a traditional hussar dress with sky blue dolman and breeches (here the riding overalls with leather reinforcement) with scarlet cuffs and collar, scarlet pelisse, and all yellow (gold for officers) braiding.

Plate 50

Hussard de l'égalité 1792 ou hussards de Boyer en 1793, 6e regiment
Hussards de Fabrefonds ou Éclaireurs de Fabrefonds 1792, en 1793 8e regiment.
Lienhart et Humbert.[68]

Hussard de l'égalité 1792
The hussards de l'égalité had as a full name 'défenseurs de la liberté et de l'égalité' (defenders of liberty and equality). They were also known as hussards de Boyer, as they were raised by citizen Gabriel Etienne Boyer on 2 September 1792 in the north of France. They became the 7e hussards on 23 November 1792, having fought at Jemmapes on 6 November. On the 6 June 1793 they were re-numbered to 6e hussards. Their uniform was entirely that of traditional hussar regiments with a full red dolman, white pelisse and blue breeches making them a colourful unit sporting the national colours.

Hussard de Fabrefonds ou éclaireurs de Fabrefonds 1792
On 10 October 1792 in Nancy, *colonel* Fabrefonds, aide de camp to général de division Kellermann, organised a unit of éclaireurs (scouts) de l'armée du centre which became known as éclaireurs de Fabrefonds. They became the 9e hussards on 26 February 1793 and were renumbered to 8e on the 10 May 1793. They incorporated other light cavalry units in June 1793.

We have mainly modern reconstructions for this unit, usually showing an all green uniform with yellow as a distinctive colour. In this case, Boisselier has followed Lienhart and Humbert which gave the unit a green dolman with a green pelisse and red breeches. This actually corresponds more to another unit, the hussards de Lamothe which was raised in November 1792 in Compiegne and fought first with Dumouriez in the north and then later in the west. That unit became the 8e hussars, later the 7e by June 1793, which could explain the confusion. Lienhart and Humbert having confused the two 8e hussars.

---

68 Equality Hussars 1792 or Boyer Hussars in 1793, 6th Regiment. Fabrefonds' Hussars or Fabrefonds' Scouts 1792, in 1793, 8th Regiment. Lienhart and Humbert. Dated July 1943.

Plate 51

Cavalier au 3e regiment de hussards 1794–1795 d'après la collection Mellinet, bibliothèque nationale Cabinet des Estampes
Cavalier au 4e regiment de hussards 1794–1795 d'après la collection Mellinet, bibliothèque nationale Cabinet des Estampes.[69]

This plate shows two hussar figures taken from the Hauck series of watercolours now in the Bibliothèque nationale de France. Hauck did these from life but did not indicate which unit they belonged to, so Boisselier attributed them to specific units based on the uniforms shown.

Cavalier au 3e regiment de hussards 1794–1795
The original watercolour by Hauck shows a much younger and elegant individual with a very tight-fitting uniform. Boisselier has somewhat aged this hussar, but otherwise his copy is quite faithful to the original. The man is in an undress French style coat and Hungarian breeches and boots. The only obvious element of hussar dress is the tricolour barrel sash. On the original watercolour the coat and breeches colour are a more a blueish grey and not as much a light blue as shown by Boisselier. This clearly points to the 3e hussards which had worn this very specific gris argentin (silvery grey). He carries an impressive hussar sabre. The wearing of a hat is typical of undress or walking-out dress. The very fancy tricolour plume is also characteristic of the period.

Cavalier au 4e regiment de hussards
Again, the colours worn; red dolman and breeches, blue pelisse point to a specific unit, in this case the 4e hussards (former colonel-général). On the original watercolour, the braiding is less opulent than on Boisselier's figure. This man is still completely in his original royal army uniform, but he has a tricolour plume to his busby and the tricolour barrel sash which unequivocally show him to be a Republican soldier.

Plate 52

2e hussards de la liberté – cavalier en pelisse, archives de la guerre et Titeux 1793
Bataillons de réquisitionnaires 8 septembre 1793, Journal Militaire et estampe de la collection Hennin, cabinet des estampes de la bibliothèque nationale.[70]

2e hussards de la liberté – cavalier en pelisse
This is, as indicated the second hussards de la liberté. It was created on 23 November 1792 at the same time as the other, first, hussards de la liberté in Paris, Beauvais, and Lille. Its creator, citizen Levasseur-Dumont was actually a con-man who took advantage of this to sell officer commissions to the highest bidders. He even claimed that his unit was the 8e hussards and had standards designed and manufactured. The poor quality of the unit led Dumouriez to dismiss Dumont and

---

[69] Trooper from the 3rd Hussar Regiment 1794–1795 from the Mellinet collection, National Library, print room. Trooper from the 4th Hussar Regiment 1794-1795 from the Mellinet collection, National Library, print room. Dated November 1943.
[70] 2nd Liberty Hussars – Trooper wearing a pelisse, war archives and Titeux 1793. Requisition Battalions 8 September 1793, Military Journal and print from the Hennin collection, print room of the National Library. Dated October 1943.

place one of his aides de camp in command. Known as the 10e hussards, it ended up being renumbered 9e by May 1793

We have archival evidence for the dress of the unit which wore a short dark blue coat with yellow braiding, with red collar and cuffs, a red waistcoat, dark blue breeches. As a headdress it had a black hussar cap with its top being red – this is probably a mirliton style cap. This is confirmed by a contemporary illustration by Gregorius. In December 1792, they adopted a sky-blue pelisse which they wore above the coat, which while being short still had the bottom of it visible with the pelisse worn over. In 1793 a regular dolman replaced the earlier coat.

Boisselier has illustrated this man according to the archives including giving him a dolman rather than the short coat which indeed dates him to 1793 and not earlier.

Bataillons de réquisitionnaires 8 septembre 1793
On 23 August 1793, the Republican government (the National Convention) published a decree 'which puts all the French into a state of permanent requisition for service in the armies until the enemies will have been chased from the territory of the republic'. This mass requisition was truly universal: young men were to go and fight, married men were to either manufacture weapons or transport supplies, women would manufacture tents, clothing or serve in hospitals, the very young would prepare bandages and the elderly would be 'carried on to public spots to entice with courage the warriors, preach hatred for the Kings and the unity of the republic.'[71]

Each district was to ensure that at first all men from the age of 18–25 would be supplied and march as a battalion under a banner on which would be written 'le peuple français contre les tyrans' (The French people against the tyrants). This initial decree was far from complete and so an instruction was written and published on 1 September 1793, followed on the 8 September by a decree ordering its execution. Its third title, or chapter, details what kind of uniform and equipment was to be supplied for these battalions of requisitioned men.

The first article logically indicated that wherever possible the men should wear the national uniform, but then the second mentions that if possible, each citizen-soldier should receive:

A pair of cloth trousers with an inner leather reinforcement
A Marseillaise style jacket made of cloth, of whichever colour could be had
A lined waistcoat
A forage cap
2 pairs of shoes
2 pairs of stockings
3 shirts
3 collars [cloth stocks]
3 brushes
2 combs
1 knapsack of hide or oilskin
1 sabre with belt

---

71 Décret qui met tous les Français en réquisition permanente pour le service des armées, jusqu'au moment où les ennemis auront été chassés du territoire de la république, du 23 août 1793, *Journal Militaire*, 1793, p.601,

The Marseillaise coat was also known as the carmagnole and was a typical revolutionary clothing item which used less fabric than the regular military coat.

Boisselier has used this description as well as contemporary prints to come up with this figure which pretty much gives us the look of the regular revolutionary citizen-soldier at the end of 1793, at the peak of the Jacobin radical revolutionary government. His dress is very much civilian. His trousers are indeed reinforced with black leather. The only true military item of dress is his forage cap which sports the national colours.

Plate 53
Trompette du 9e hussards vers 1798 d'après Rugendas Bibliothèque Nationale
Officier du 7e bis de hussards vers 1796 d'après une estampe du temps.[72]

Trompette du 9e hussards vers 1798
Although the 9e hussards did not have any trace of yellow as a distinctive colour, it seems its trumpeters wore a yellow dolman for quite some time. Is this due to the fact that at some stage the 9e was the hussards de Fabrefonds whose distinctive colour was yellow, and its trumpeters wore a yellow dolman and pelisse? This is possible but is a far-fetched hypothesis. In any case, later on during the Empire, the 9e continued to have its trumpeters dressed in a yellow dolman and pelisse.

Here the source used by Boisselier is a Rugendas print which is strictly contemporary and he copied it in detail. The man also has a tricolour plume and barrel sash in typical Republican fashion.

Officier du 7e bis de hussards vers 1796
Boisselier indicated that his source was a contemporary print, which is too vague to actually trace. We have the Margerand reconstructions, the Marbot plates but also Devernois' memoirs as a former officer in this regiment. All confirm what this plate shows.

The 7e bis was created from several units as we have seen earlier: the first formation of the hussards de la liberté, but also the partisans de l'armée du Rhin and two squadrons from the 7e hussards. It adopted a very smart hussar uniform with red dolman, blue pelisse, and breeches. The 7e bis is well known as it fought in Italy under Bonaparte and then was chosen along with the 22e chasseurs à cheval to be the only light cavalry units in Egypt. On its return from Egypt in 1803 it was, much to the dismay of its men, transformed into the 28e dragons.

According to a contemporary painting showing the 7e bis hussars in Italy, the men also wore an early type of shako with a detachable visor and had a gold 7 and a small B denoted on their sabretache.

---

72 Trumpeter of the 9th Hussars circa 1798 after Rugendas, National Library. Officer of the 7th bis Hussars circa 1796 after a contemporary print. Dated December 1943.

Plate 54
1er Médecin 1798 d'après le recueil de Valmont – Bibliothèque Nationale
Conducteur des équipages du service de santé, recueil de Lienhart et Humbert.[73]

The next two plates are devoted to medical services during the late revolutionary period.

The Revolution and Empire period saw a major development of military medical services. This was due both to the obvious need for such efficient support given the volume and scope of fighting over almost a quarter of a century but also thanks to the presence of some remarkable individuals whose science and impact went beyond just the army.

Percy and Larrey were surgeons who practiced with excellence on the field of battle but also improved surgery techniques and organisation. Desgenettes, as a physician, also did much to improve medical treatment. Many left memoirs and works which shared not only their general experience of those turbulent times, but also their medical observations and practice, and which remained required reading to train doctors and surgeons throughout the nineteenth century.

At the end of the monarchy, the medical services were already well organised and medical officers had a regulated uniform. They were considered officers as they carried a sword, symbol of their officer status. They however had their own specific ranking system and compensation and did not wear epaulettes as regular army officers usually did. The initial coat colour for medical officers at the end of the monarchy and until 1796 was light grey with black velvet cuffs, no coat lapels. Depending on their rank they had various gold braiding at the buttonholes.

In 1796, the colour was altered to grey with a blueish tint. Distinctive colours were introduced for the coat, still without any lapels, at the collar and cuffs. Physicians were to wear black velvet and have a grey waistcoat. Surgeons were to have crimson velvet and a scarlet waistcoat. Pharmacists were to have dark green velvet and a scarlet waistcoat. Again, braiding varied according to the ranks. We have little iconographic evidence for that period, except for paintings done later and representing battles during the first Italian campaign. These show that the blueish grey colour was used but, as for all revolutionary troops, there was quite some diversity in coat cuts and overall aspect. In one case a senior surgeon is shown wearing a dark blue coat of the same colour and cut as the army staff but with dark red velvet collar and cuffs and the relevant braiding.

On 7 August 1798, a new regulation was issued which lasted until 1803. The medical officers now adopted the usual French-style coat of national blue colour with 1/32 white thread in the fabric. It had lapels, a turned down collar and cuffs. The previous distinctive colours were retained and worn at collar, cuffs and lapels.

Physicians wore black velvet, with waistcoat and breeches the same colour as the coat, and a white waistcoat for summer dress. Surgeons wore crimson velvet, with breeches the same colour as the coat, and a red waistcoat, or white for summer dress. Pharmacists wore bottle green velvet, with breeches same colour as the coat, and a scarlet waistcoat, or white for summer dress.

First class medical officers with an army had seven braids on each lapel, two on each side of the collar, two on each cuff, and three on the pocket flap. Second class medical officers had no braids on the lapels, but two on each side of the collar and cuffs. Third class medical officers had only two braids on each side of the collar. The plume on the hat was to be red with a black tip. This uniform was universal, except that medical officers attached to a unit would wear the button of that unit.

73　1st Physician 1798 from Valmont's collection – National Library. Medical service driver, Lienhart and Humbert collection. Dated October 1943.

1er Médecin 1798
Boisselier has copied this figure from a Valmont watercolour. It follows very much the 1798 regulation except for some details. There are three braids on each cuff which was probably seen as more appropriate and was later confirmed with the 1803 regulation. The waistcoat is white as per summer dress, and the breeches are not blue which, again seem more in line with the usual fashion of the period. The plume is indeed black and red but with black in the middle.

Conducteur des équipages du service de santé
This medical services train driver is taken from the Lienhart and Humbert volumes. Train services were actually handled by private companies under contract with the armies. Their personnel were militarised in the sense that they were subject to military discipline and provided with a uniform of some kind. This latter part was however left outside of military regulations as this was handled by the company under contract.

We do however know from contemporary sources that such men would be dressed in colours that were not in favour with the military: often brown and sometimes grey. This is the case with this man who wears a short military style brown coat with black cuffs and turned down collar. This may actually be a reference to the black distinctive colour worn by all medical officers prior to 1796. He has leather reinforced trousers which is logical for someone riding horses. These men were usually armed only with a short sabre and no firearms.

Plate 55
Pharmacien 1798, d'après le recueil de Valmont bibliothèque nationale
Chirurgien Major 1798, d'après le recueil de Valmont bibliothèque nationale.[74]

This plate is the continuation of the previous one. Again, Valmont is the source and it is consistent in showing the same discrepancies versus the 1798 regulation: three braids on the cuffs, black and red plume with black in the middle, and white waistcoat and breeches. The man on the left is a pharmacist probably a second class one (as the cuffs are not visible). The man on the right is a *chirurgien major* – a first class surgeon (chief surgeon) attached to a unit.

In 1803, the uniform reverted to a coat with no lapels. Its colour became the famous bleu barbeau (pike blue) which is actually a medium blue, barely lighter than the blue shown on this plate. Given campaign conditions, it would tend to become a still lighter blue.

The same distinctive colours were kept and are still used to this day in the French army. The only difference is that surgeons and physicians now both wear crimson velvet while pharmacists have kept green.

---

74 Pharmacist 1798, after the Valmont collection, National Library. Surgeon Major 1798, after the Valmont collection, National Library. Dated October 1943.

Plate 56
Canonnier de Marine de 17re classe 1796–1802 Valmont
Compagnie des 'hommes de couleur' 1798–1800 Valmont.[75]

This last plate is devoted to two fairly exotic topics related to the navy. Both have been copied by Boisselier from Valmont and are actually in volume 15 (out of the 18 present) which are in the Bibliothèque nationale de France.

Canonnier de Marine de 17re classe 1796–1802
As indicated previously, naval artillery became a branch of its own in 1792. The two original regiments were reorganised into seven demi-brigades which were transferred to the army. They were to stay part of the army until formally disbanded in 1814 and immediately re-created as the Corps royal des artilleurs de la marine.

Nothing really distinguishes this man at a distance from his counterpart in the army foot artillery. The biggest difference are the buttons which had an anchor and are of course not visible on this plate. Boisselier did not exactly copy the Valmont figure as he has given this man white leather equipment. In fact, on the Valmont watercolour, as with the previous figure shown on plate 22, the leather equipment is all black as was usually the case for naval personnel. This distinction was to remain as even later period sources show naval artillery troops in Germany in 1813 with black leather cartridge and sabre belts.

Compagnie des 'hommes de couleur' 1798–1800
This is a rather unknown and ill-documented unit. In 1797, when the peace of Campo-Formio was signed, Great Britain released the prisoners of war that had been captured including those taken in the West Indies in 1793 (Martinique) and 1796 (Sainte-Lucie). Those troops had been raised from the local population with European officers. Upon their return, the men of colour were separated from their officers and regrouped on the Ile d'Aix (an island off the mid-Atlantic coast) where they were organised into two compagnies des hommes de couleur. They were claimed by the ministry of the navy as colonial troops and except for a small group which was sent to Senegal, they were sent back to the West Indies.

Apart from the watercolour by Valmont we have no other source for their uniform. They were clearly dressed in a naval type uniform, all blue except for the turnbacks which were white and the red collar and piping. Black leather equipment was also given as fairly standard in the navy. The gaiters on the original Valmont watercolour are even shorter and more reminiscent of light infantry.

---

75 Naval gunner 17th class 1796-1802, Valmont. Company of 'men of colour' 1798-1800 Valmont. Dated December 1943.

4

Conclusion

'Citizens, the revolution is set upon the principles which started it; it is finished!'
The Consuls of the Republic, 24 frimaire year 8 (15 December 1799)

On 9 November 1799 (18 brumaire year 8), *général de division* Napoleon Bonaparte had seized power with a dashing coup. France was still a republic in name, but the executive branch of its government now took the form of a powerful triumvirate, the three consuls. One, the first consul, had more power than the others, and he was none other than Bonaparte.

Thanks to his military victory at Marengo and that of Moreau at Hohenlinden, peace was at hand with the continental enemies of France by the end of 1800. Following the defeat of the armée d'Orient in Egypt in 1801, peace could be signed with the last remaining hostile country, Great Britain. This was done at Amiens on 25 March 1802.

A little less than 10 years after the start of the Revolutionary Wars, peace had come back to Europe. None could yet foresee that within a little over a year, hostilities would renew between France and Britain. For the time being, British visitors could once again travel to and through France. Scions of good families could, as under the monarchy go on a grand tour which included as one of its highlights, Paris and the French countryside.

Such was the case for a young man who destined himself to the clergy, Edward Stanley, son of a baronet and freshly out of St John's College, Cambridge. In June 1802 he landed in Rouen, Normandy and from there proceeded through Paris, to Lyon on his way to Switzerland and then Italy. While in France he wrote letters to his parents and brother, chronicling what he saw and witnessed.

At that time, young Stanley could not imagine that he would come back to France only 12 years later, following Napoleon's first abdication in 1814 and yet again a year later, after Waterloo. Then again, he would write letters which have become classics for any student of the 1814–1815 period as they describe Paris before and after Waterloo. Yet, his much earlier writings in 1802 are of even more interest as they give us an outsider's view of post-revolutionary France and provide the reader with an apt conclusion to this volume.

Throughout his 1802 travel, Stanley discovered a country which showed obvious signs of disruption, destruction, extreme poverty: 'I never before saw such strong marks of poverty both in the houses and inhabitants.' But he was quick to notice that some buildings were better kept than others. In the same letter at the early start of his trip he wrote: 'The only buildings at all tolerable are the barracks, which in general are large and well taken care of, and plenty of them are in every town and village. Every person here is a Soldier, ready to turn out at a moment's warning.'[1]

More than anything else, Stanley discovered that French society had become almost totally militarized. He would encounter officers and men at theatres, not only as spectators, but also keeping an eye out for any sign of unruliness. One Frenchman was bold enough to utter that 'if he were in England, he would do as he pleases', understating that, being in France, he could not. In Rouen, he also had dinner with a party of five officers at a table d'hôtes: 'In my life I never saw such ill-bred blackguards, dirty in their way of eating, overbearing in their conversation.' He travelled from Rouen to Paris in a stagecoach which was escorted by a party of dragoons and regularly he saw parties of infantrymen on watch along the road. All this on account of robbers and the need to restore security. Once in Paris, again he could not but observe militarization as he wrote to his brother: 'Paris, like all the country swarms with soldiers; in every street there is a barrack. In Paris alone there are upwards of 15 thousand men. I must say nothing of the government. It is highly necessary in France for every person, particularly Strangers to be careful in delivering their opinions.' Interestingly, a few days before, he had written to his parents about Bonaparte that: 'he is a fine fellow by all accounts; a Military Government when such a head as his manages everything cannot be a Grievance. Indeed it is productive of so much order and regularity that I begin not to dislike it so much.'[2]

Young Stanley's accounts provide proof that France had massively changed due to the revolution and the need it had had to defend it and itself as a nation. 'Citizens to arms' was just not a verse in a song, but a reality lived by everyone in France. Such militarization was, of course, alien to Edward Stanley and his compatriots. He perceived with accuracy how easy it had been for a military government to install itself and how beneficial it could be to a country which had gone through such massive upheaval over a decade.

From these few years of peace, France became a totally militarized and disciplined country ready to undertake conquests under and for its leader, the Emperor.

The revolutionary armies were indeed the cradle of the Napoleonic forces, in spirit, means, and as this volume has tried to show, uniforms.

---

1   Jane H. Adfane and Maud Grenfell (eds), *Before and After Waterloo, Letters from Edward Stanley, 1802, 1814, 1816* (London: Unwin, 1907), pp.27–28.
2   Adfane and Grenfell (eds), *Before and After Waterloo*, pp.30–40.

Sources, Bibliography, and Further Reading

This chapter is intended not only to provide the reader with the list of sources the author has consulted and used, but also as a guide and an incentive for further personal research. Sources are divided into texts and iconography.

Texts

In English
British and American historians have been very active in the last decades on the military aspect of the French revolutionary armies, more so than their French counterparts. Three volumes stand out and are actually quoted in modern French historical works:

Alan Forrest, *The Soldiers of the French Revolution* (London: Duke University Press, 1990)
John A. Lynn, *The Bayonets of the Republic: Motivation and Tactics in the Army of Revolutionary France 1791–1794* (London: Routledge, 2019 (originally published 1996))
Paddy Griffith, *The Art of War of Revolutionary France 1789–1802* (London: Greenhill, 1998)

In French
Reference texts on uniforms and organisation:

Malibran
Commonly known as the *Malibran*, its official title is the 'guide à l'usage des artistes et des costumiers contenant la description des uniformes de l'armée française de 1780 à 1848'. This massive (close to a thousand pages) volume was published in 1904 and was the work of M. Malibran, a retired civil works engineer. With infinite patience he went through all the regulation texts and more from 1780 to 1848 to provide, by branch of service and unit, a detailed description of uniforms worn. This text volume was completed a few years later with a volume of plates giving line drawings for the main items described. Although quite dry reading, it is extremely informative and is the first work to look up if one is fluent enough in French. From there one can confirm and complete with other sources. A similar and earlier work is the Lienhart and Humbert but given its numerous colour plates, this is listed in the iconography section.

Le Journal Militaire

The basic source for anyone researching the organisation, uniforms and equipment of the French army from 1790 into the nineteenth century is the *Journal Militaire*. This publication actually started in 1790 as a private endeavour aiming to provide all those interested with regular comprehensive information on military administration and debates. This regular journal established itself quickly as a quasi-official publication. Between the regular issues and the supplements published after 1799 to cover what had been missed earlier, it covers pretty much all that was officially published in terms of laws, decrees, decisions and more, for both the French army and navy. Full collections can be found in large public libraries. The revolutionary period volumes can be found online if one is patient enough to hunt them down!

Memoirs

The entire 1789–1815 period abounds with memoirs of all kinds. In regard to the revolutionary period, there were two large waves of publication. The first in the 1830s and 1840s when veterans of the Napoleonic Wars published their 'souvenirs' which often included the revolutionary period. The second wave was around the centennial year of 1889 and up to 1914 when historians and intellectuals hunted down unknown manuscripts from public or family archives and published them. Founded in 1893 the military association La Sabretache contributed to this by publishing throughout its history many such memoirs.

The best memoirs are those written exactly at the time of the events like a journal or letters.

Many of the references below are available only from either Google Books or the Bibliothèque nationale de France digital service (gallica.bnf.fr).

Baron Ernouf, *Souvenirs militaires d'un jeune abbé, soldat de la république 1793–1801* (Paris: Didier, 1881)
L. Larchey, *journal de marche d'un volontaire de 1792* (Paris: Fricasse 1882)
J. Lombard, *Un volontaire de 1792* (Paris: Mireur, 1892)
Vallet & Parisée, *Carnet d'étapes du Dragon Marquant, démarches et étapes de l'armée du centre pendant la campagne de 1792* (Paris-Nancy: Berger-Levrault 1898)
F. Funck-Brentano, *Joliclerc, volontaire aux armées de la révolution* (Paris: Perrin, 1905)
M. Mangerel, *Le capitaine Gerbaud 1773–1799* (Paris: Plon, 1910)
A. Chuquet, *Lettres de 1793* (Paris: Honoré Champion, 1911)
G. Noël, *Au temps des volontaires – lettres d'un volontaire de 1792* (Paris: Plon, 1912)
Colonel Ernest Picard, *Au service de la Nation, lettres de volontaires (1792–1798)* (Paris: Librairie Félix Alcan 1914)

Studies

The end of the nineteenth century was ripe with excellent in-depth publications. The celebration of the 1789 centennial in 1889 was of course the occasion to undertake such works, but even greater was the motivation to analyse and study past military successes so as to prepare for the certain future war of revenge with Germany.

C. Rousset, *Les volontaires 1791–1794* (Paris: Didier, 1870) – the original work on volunteers and still a useful reference
H. Choppin, *Notes sur l'organisation de l'armée pendant la révolution, 1er août 1789–30 octobre 1795* (Paris: Tanera, 1873)

D'Hauterive, *L'armée sous la révolution 1789–1794* (Paris: Ollendorf, 1894)
Chassin & Hennet, *Les volontaires nationaux pendant la révolution* (Paris: Cerf, Noblet, Quantin 1899–1906) – a massive three volume reference work on Parisian volunteers
G. Dumon, l*es bataillons de volontaires nationaux* (Paris: Lavauzelle, 1914)

There is a series devoted to cavalry with a large emphasis on the revolutionary period which was published at the beginning on the twentieth century.

Édouard Desbrière, *La cavalerie de 1740 à 1789* (Paris-Nancy: Berger-Levrault, 1906)
Édouard Desbrière, *La cavalerie pendant la Révolution, du 14 juillet 1789 au 26 juin 1794* (Paris-Nancy: Berger-Levrault, 1907)
Édouard Desbrière, *La cavalerie pendant la révolution la fin de la Convention du 19 juin 1794 au 27 octobre 1795* (Paris-Nancy: Berger-Levrault, 1908)
Édouard Desbrière, *La cavalerie sous le Directoire* (Paris-Nancy: Berger-Levrault, 1910)

After 1914, military history studies on the eighteenth and nineteenth centuries were no longer a focus. The imperial period was a much more consensual topic. The advent of the nouvelle histoire, which considered military history of no importance unlike social and economic trends, made such works unpopular. One work does stand out from that period though:

H. Lachouque, *aux armes citoyens* (Paris: Perrin, 1969). The great Napoleonic historian Henry Lachouque wrote this rather simple but comprehensive volume which is a great one-volume introduction to the military history of the revolution.

As of the 1970s, the late Jean-Paul Bertaud who was instrumental in the renewal of French military history started publishing updated studies on the French revolutionary armies.

Jean-Paul Bertaud, *La Révolution armée. les soldats-citoyens et la Révolution française* (Paris: Robert Laffont, 1979)
Jean-Paul Bertaud, *La Vie quotidienne des soldats de la révolution* (Paris: Hachette, 1985) – a nice one volume work part of a very popular series on daily life.
Jean-Paul Bertaud, *Valmy* (Paris: Gallimard, 1970, 1989, 2013).

The last volume is almost essential reading as it both describes the Valmy campaign and events, but more importantly really updates research on the revolutionary armies. Regularly updated, it is best to go with the 2013 edition.

Sources Chapter 2

On Cambronne:
The famous Waterloo general did not attract many biographers. The basic reference remains:
Leon Brunschvicg, *Cambronne* (Nantes: Vier, 1894)

The latest biography is:
Stephane Calvet, *Cambronne, la légende de Waterloo* (Paris: Vendémiaire, 2016).

This is a nice short volume and an enjoyable read.

On Lejeune:
The main source is of course his own memoirs *Souvenirs d'un officier de l'empire* published in 1851. The other source for the artist volunteers can be found in the Chassin & Hennet publication on Parisian volunteers (see above).

On Desvernois:
Desvernois first published a summarized version of his memoirs which is of very little interest. A full version is Albert Dufourcq, *Mémoires du général Baron Desvernois* (Paris: Plon, 1898). It is one of the most enjoyable memoirs to have come down to us from the 1789–1815 period.

On Women-Soldiers/Volunteers:
The main sources used were found in the military archives in Vincennes (SHD) where the 1Yi series lists the files devoted to 'women soldiers'.
   File 1Yi-10 is that of Angélique Duchemin and it is the largest of all.
   The other anecdotes were found in the journal *La revolution française, revue d'histoire moderne et contemporaine*. In its July 1904 issue, there is an article by F. Gernaux 'les femmes soldats pendant la révolution', followed by another article by Léon Deschamps in the October 1904 issue, 'les femmes soldats dans la Sarthe'. Both articles clearly demonstrate that there were far more women soldiers than those whose files have survived in the French military archives at SHD. This publication can be found online and its interest is not limited to those articles!

Iconography

The author has relied in great part on his own collection of contemporary iconography accumulated over the years. However, as one cannot have everything, he also has resorted over the years to consulting large public libraries. Here are the main ones to look up for someone wishing to study the matter.

The Anne S.K. Brown Military Collection, Brown University, Providence, Rhode Island, USA[1]
It should come as no surprise that this institution is mentioned first. Ms Brown collected over her lifetime the largest collection of military iconography. Although not all of it has been digitised and made available online, much of it is. Amongst its treasures, one can find Hoffmann plates, but also numerous contemporary works by Seele, Rugendas, Hauck and many others.

Bibliothèque nationale de France (BNF)
This institution has inherited its collections from the old Royal and then Imperial library. It has been housing volumes since the seventeenth century and, although its aim is a general one, it does have in its prints and graphic arts section, a large selection of military related iconography. It specifically houses some important collections:

---

[1] <https://repository.library.brown.edu/studio/collections/bdr:224400/>

The de Vinck collection is a wide collection of prints related to French history.

The Hennin collection which was compiled during the nineteenth century and has some exceptional (and sometimes unique) works. Boisselier made much use of it, as indicated in the text.

The de Ridder collection which entered the BNF in 1945–1946. Given this date, Boisselier could not have used it for this series, but the de Ridder collection is specifically devoted to military uniforms and many volumes have been digitised and made available online via Gallica. De Ridder was a very large and wealthy collector who spoke many different languages and had multiple areas of interest both in terms of periods and countries.

Some specific series are worth checking out but on site at the library as they are not available online (except for OA-105):
OA-102c: Valmont's 18 volumes devoted to French uniforms, Volume 5 covers the revolutionary periods with a few more figures in volume 15 (Navy)
OA-102x and OA-102y: Raffet's son's large volumes of various watercolours and copies he made from various sources and collections
OA-105: Three exquisite volumes by Hoffmann showing the royal army in 1786–1788
ZF-209-4: The 'Mellinet album' – Hauck's splendid watercolours done from life in 1794–1795 in Holland. This volume is not readily available on site and must be pre-requested and its consultation must be justified.

Also worthy of note: the OA-21–8 volume has various prints and works on the revolution, as well as OA-101 and OA-101a. There are some very rare Hoffmann prints in these various collections.

The Bibliothèque nationale de France has an excellent general catalogue available online (https://catalogue.bnf.fr/index.do).

It also manages the excellent Gallica website (https://gallica.bnf.fr) which is a major resource for any researcher in any field as it gives direct access to much of its collection and allows downloads.

The Carnavalet Museum
The Musée de l'histoire de Paris, better known as 'Carnavalet' is considered the unofficial museum of the French revolution. As the revolution was mainly a Parisian event, it is quite logical that it houses an exceptional collection of artefacts, paintings, and documents all related to those events. Many of these are visible (and downloadable at high resolution) online through the digital library of Paris museums (https://www.parismuseescollections.paris.fr/en)

Without doubt the most famous, and precious collection within Carnavalet is that of the 'Lesueur gouaches'. Probably executed by Jean-François Lesueur for a puppet-show type of theatrical representation, these have been preserved by Lesueur's family. Although the bulk of the collection seems to be now in the museum, some may still be in private or family hands. These extremely fine original works chronicle most of the revolution and show the people of Paris with an incredible wealth of detail. They are an exceptional source on the Garde nationale de Paris, volunteers and other units. Although Boisselier does not seem to have used them directly, they have had an influence on all later artists who represented the revolution. They are also well known to many of the French as they have been extensively used in history books.

Les Invalides, or rather the Paris *musée de l'armée*

It holds an extensive collection of iconography in between its library and its prints and paintings departments. Boisselier was a frequent visitor to this institution. Back in his days, it was fairly easy for a known artist such as him, to simply sift through the various collections and volumes which were all readily available on site and to which he was obviously granted liberal access. This is of course today much less the case due to obvious preservation considerations. Researchers are of course welcome and the staff both of the library and prints department are immensely helpful and friendly. However, much of the collections have been moved to the Versailles suburbs due to reasons of space and better conservation. Also, some collections like the Vanson collection have not been kept as a collection but classified more logically by chronology. This is also the case for the Dubois de l'Estang collection. In fact, Boisselier made good use of both the Vanson and Dubois de l'Estang collections to create his own series on the French revolution. Today Les Invalides and its library and prints departments remains a wonderful source for anyone wishing to study the period and especially its uniforms.

Vincennes

The Service Historique de la Défense (SHD) in Vincennes is where the French military archives are stored. It also has a library with an expanding military uniforms section. There is however not much devoted to the revolution per se except for Bagetti's wonderful watercolours on the first campaign in Italy. These can be consulted on line on the *mémoire des hommes* web site (https://www.memoiredeshommes.sga.defense.gouv.fr). The SHD is of course an incredible source for primary archival research, as indicated above when this author researched women soldiers.

Who were the main artists?

The revolutionary period abounds with many individual prints and series. Listing all of them would require a volume in itself, but here are the main artists who produced series which Boisselier used:

Nicolas (Niklaus) Hoffmann: a native of Germany, Hoffmann was born in 1740. He settled in Paris around 1774 at the request of his employer, the elector of Hessen-Darmstadt. For him he extensively documented military uniforms. Unfortunately, that production was lost in the destructions of the Second World War. Yet, fortunately for us, Hoffmann also produced commissions for local customers and prints for casual clients, and many of these did survive the war. He would typically produce a fine black and white print which he would then adapt and colour according to the subject. He also drew and painted individual works, such as specific portraits. Thanks to him we have a remarkable documentation on the royal army at the end of the 1780s, but also wonderful images showing the Garde nationale de Paris but also local Gardes nationaux and many other types of the revolutionary period.

Hauck: a Dutch artist who was active in the mid-1790s. He did an extensive series of watercolours showing Pichegru's army. Some of them he also produced as extremely fine coloured prints. These are one of the main sources on the early armies of the French revolution.

Rovatti: Rovatti was a priest in Modena who undertook a quasi-daily chronicle of his town, illustrating it. He thus showed the various troops of the first Italian campaign in a naïve but detailed way. His 'cronaca' is still in Modena and can be consulted online (https://lodovico.medialibrary.it)

Rugendas: a member of a long line of artists, Johann Lorenz Rugendas produced many coloured prints showing battles and events of the Revolutionary Wars. The quality of details is sometimes exceptional, and he has often been used as a source.

There were many other German artists like Rugendas: Kobell, and Seele, not to mention all the other anonymous ones who have left us with prints which are almost photographic snapshots of French troops in Germany.

Further Reading

For someone wishing to pursue further the topic of the French revolutionary army with modern, easier to access sources, both from a strict uniforms/iconographic perspective but also in terms of organisational and military history, here are some suggestions.

Helion offers several excellent titles on the period, amongst these, the following stand out:

Terry Crowdy, *French Light Infantry 1784–1815*. This is Terry's pet topic on which he has authored several other volumes with other publishers (and two volumes on infantry with Osprey). Excellent primary research.

Pierre-Baptiste Guillemot, *The Garde nationale 1789–1815*. Pierre-Baptiste is a brilliant up and coming young French historian who is focused on the 1789–1815 period, but even more so on the revolution in its military aspect. This work is ground-breaking in that no volumes on the Garde nationale for that period had yet been written.

The cercle français de la figurine historique (CFFH) is a small association of French military miniatures enthusiasts which regularly publishes excellent volumes on little-known topics. In 2020 it published *légions et corps français des années terribles 1792–1796* by the late Didier Davin. This was Didier Davin's core topic on which he had produced many articles for both the CFFH and his own association Le Bivouac, a southern group. Given that the title referred to the terrible years of 1792–1796, it seemed logical that a second volume on 1797–1801 should have followed. Unfortunately, Didier Davin passed away a few months before the publication of this first work. This author is quite indebted to all the work done by him as he has used both this one publication and many of his other articles to cross-reference or track sources.

Finally, there are two 'old' volumes which are still fairly easily available as used books and are recommended.

For the English speaking public: Philip Haythornwaite, *Uniforms of the French Revolutionary Wars 1789–1802* (London: Blandford, 1981). This popular volume, illustrated by Christopher Warner, is a good introduction and has the benefit of also showing the enemies of revolutionary France.

The best 'old' work is however in French and is by the well-known Liliane and Fred Funcken: *Les soldats de la révolution française*, (Tournai: Casterman, 1988). Published in time for the bicentennial, this was the last of the superb Funcken series of books. In a somewhat odd, but more modern format, it is probably their best. Very well researched, using extensive primary sources (including Lesueur's gouaches), it is less known than their other works and unfortunately did not have the success of the others.

From Reason to Revolution – Warfare 1721-1815

http://www.helion.co.uk/series/from-reason-to-revolution-1721-1815.php

The 'From Reason to Revolution' series covers the period of military history 1721–1815, an era in which fortress-based strategy and linear battles gave way to the nation-in-arms and the beginnings of total war.

This era saw the evolution and growth of light troops of all arms, and of increasingly flexible command systems to cope with the growing armies fielded by nations able to mobilise far greater proportions of their manpower than ever before. Many of these developments were fired by the great political upheavals of the era, with revolutions in America and France bringing about social change which in turn fed back into the military sphere as whole nations readied themselves for war. Only in the closing years of the period, as the reactionary powers began to regain the upper hand, did a military synthesis of the best of the old and the new become possible.

The series examines the military and naval history of the period in a greater degree of detail than has hitherto been attempted, and has a very wide brief, with the intention of covering all aspects from the battles, campaigns, logistics, and tactics, to the personalities, armies, uniforms, and equipment.

Submissions

The publishers would be pleased to receive submissions for this series. Please email reasontorevolution@helion.co.uk, or write to Helion & Company Limited, Unit 8 Amherst Business Centre, Budbrooke Road, Warwick, CV34 5WE

You may also be interested in:

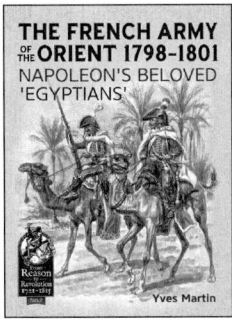

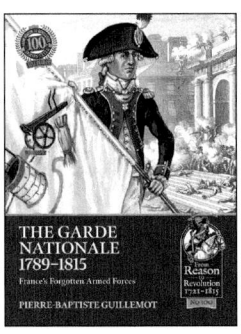

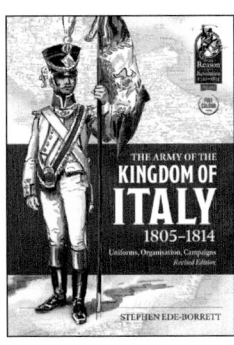

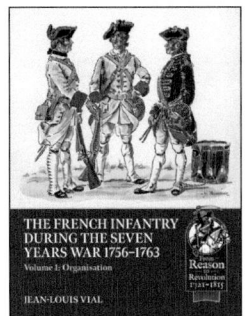